Silk Diary

An Artist's Journey from Moscow to Mendocino

An Artist's Journey from Moscow to Mendocino

Natasha Foucault

Jeanne-Michele Salander

WINTER PALACE PRESS

SAN FRANCISCO, CALIFORNIA

First published in the United States of America by
Winter Palace Press

ISBN 0-9777752-0-8

Library of Congress Control Number (LCCN) 2006923569

Edited by Corinna Fales and Keith K. Howell
Designed by Virginia Lindsay
Production coordinated by Keith K. Howell
Proofread by Donna Gillespie
Cover photography by Anton Orlov

Printed in China
in association with Prepress Assembly, Inc.
San Francisco, California

First Printing 2006

Bulk rates available.
Contact:

WINTER PALACE PRESS
1690 HAYES STREET, SAN FRANCISCO, CA 94117
1-877-848-2240

Contents

Acknowledgments

From

Natasha Foucault

First of all, I must thank my parents, Ada and Boris—I know you would have preferred a chemist or an engineer for a daughter. But once I declared my intention to be an artist, you believed in me unflaggingly, and helped me attend the most prestigious art school in the Soviet Union. And to my Grandmother: you were unable to follow your dream of being an artist, but you were my biggest supporter, paying for my art classes and encouraging me every step of the way.

To Vasin, my charismatic teacher, thank you for your "tough love" art lessons, and for insisting we never use colors directly from the tube.

To the dozens of friends and associates who have loyally supported me—helping me with my fashion shows and festival booths, and buying my wearable art and paintings whenever you could afford to—a never-ending hug of gratitude.

Thanks also go out to Michael Katz of Rupert Gibbon & Spider, Ellen and Stu of Qualin, and Deedee Shute of Exotic Silks: your generous patronage and help in expanding my art business have sustained me over many years.

And finally, thank you to my husband, Steve, for not giving me too hard a time for the hundreds of hours I spent working on this book, instead of being with you and Misha. I know you thought the project was sheer folly and madness, but at least you didn't disown me.

From

Jeanne-Michele Salander

To my parents, Carolyn and Michel: thank you for passing down to me a helpful combination of New England practicality and artistic creativity. Wish you could have read *Silk Diary*.

To dear old Miss Manning, my 9th grade English teacher: you marked up my essays with so many "Awk! Awk!" marks (for awkward) that the pages looked as if they had been attacked by a very literate parrot; but you and Warriner's little grammar book served me well.

To my best friend, Diane Curran: thank you for your intelligence, your sense of humor, and your example of courage in the face of adversity. We started our career as writers sitting in huge cardboard shipping boxes on my parents' front porch, sending messages to each other on a string. After making five murals together in the fifth grade illustrating America's pioneer days, we were artists, too.

To Bob Lewis: teacher, writer, photographer, and human being extraordinaire: you taught me passionately to love Russian language and history, and I've still not recovered.

To Deedee Shute, owner of Exotic Silks: thank you for your decades-long support and love.

Our editors, Corinna Fales and Keith Howell, were brilliant in their eagle-eye search for problems, and steadfast in their belief in *Silk Diary*; after Corinna's expert editing and encouragement, I was finally able to say, "I am a writer."

To our talented designer, Ginny Lindsay: we thank you for your never-ending patience when your fledgling authors required a lot of hand-holding.

And finally, to my husband, Chris, for your steady support of me, sequestered hour after hour with the computer terminal and The Book: your faith in me and my abilities sustains me through all the difficult life passages and self-doubts.

Introduction

Ever since I was an art student in Moscow, I had wanted to write a book. I was excited about my world, about beauty and love, and about my impressions of everything around me. The intensity of what I was feeling was pent up inside me, like a volcano about to erupt. Although I decided to focus on building my skills as a visual artist, I have faithfully kept a diary since I was a young girl. Fortunately, I was able to bring my Russian diaries with me when I made my home in California.

Several years ago, as I reflected on the body of my work, I realized that I was indeed telling the story of my life, but through the medium of painting on silk. However, the urge to write about myself was still strong.

People often ask why I chose a particular building to paint, or what it was like in Holland or growing up in the Soviet Union. There is almost never enough time to tell the whole story; but occasionally, when there is, the listener seems fascinated, and wants to hear more tales of my travels.

My co-author, Jeanne-Michele, told me that after she saw my slide show at a weekend retreat, and heard a participant casually mention that I should write a book, it appeared in her mind's eye, fully realized. She was eager to help me begin weaving together the paintings and stories so that the words and images enhanced each other. We both felt that the buildings and watery reflections were not just illustrations, but guideposts marking my journey as an artist—symbols which encoded the stories which would accompany them in *Silk Diary*.

The worst possible life for me would have been one with a predictable path, such as the relative safety of marrying a professional man early in life and raising a family. In contrast to many of my contemporaries, I thrive on making life choices for which I do not know the outcomes, preferring to leave the results of my decisions to the luck of the draw. As you will see, this willingness to take risks and to gamble with fate has given me many opportunities for adventures.

Nevertheless, I always have a safety net of Russian friends to support me along the way. Early in our lives, sharing a communal kitchen with five other families, for instance, we all learned to cooperate and help each other out. With travel restricted and hotels too expensive for most of us in the Soviet Union, we would sleep on each others' couches, showing our appreciation by bringing a small gift for the family. Armed with a little notebook of names and numbers, I still depend on a circle of friends—and friends of friends—to enliven my travel experiences.

If you are entertained or informed as you read these stories, so much the better. Although much of my life took place against a backdrop of tumultuous changes in the Soviet Union, I was concentrating only on my life as an artist—almost oblivious to the events developing around me. The fall of the Soviet Union and its effect on the Russian people is the subject of a different sort of book.

Above all, what I most want to communicate is a passion for life, for beauty, and for art without any justification for its creation. When I paint images on wearable art pieces in the style of my favorite artists, it is not to be trendy and hip, but because I love art endlessly. And because I am dedicated to transmitting my love of art, I have taught children all my life.

I have come to believe, though, that most importantly, the paintings of an artist serve as mirrors into the viewers' souls. May these mirrors reflect not so much me, but you, and help you to remember your life journey and inspire you to tell your stories. The reward will be that my devotion to silk painting will set you on creative fire.

—*Natasha Foucault*

About Painting on Silk

After a life-threatening illness in my native Russia, I could no longer work with the toxic chemicals of etching and ceramics, my favorite media, without seriously threatening my health. The relative safety of silk painting materials allowed me to continue to be an artist, and the colors flowing across the silk captivated me so thoroughly that, since then, I have never seriously considered working in any other medium.

The *gutta serti* method of painting on silk was first developed in Indonesia, where *gutta percha,* a natural latex, is harvested from the pallaquium tree. Wax resist techniques had been used for Asian batiks for thousands of years, but the gutta resist allowed the artist to create batik-like effects without immersing the fabric in several baths of different dye colors. The gutta resist is applied to tautly stretched lengths of silk with a pipette (or squeeze bottle with a metal tip) to form areas which surround and separate the areas of dyed silk. "Serti" in French means "set," as in a jewel mounted in a setting.

It's not known how silk painting found its way to Europe, but silk painters from France and Hungary believe their teachers learned the craft in France from Russians who fled there after the Revolution. The specialized dyes that were developed in France for the silk industry are now used by silk painting artists worldwide.

For my fine art, I exclusively use the color palette of Jacquard Red Label dyes. The blues, greens, and reds are similar to what I found in my water color tubes in Russia, and lend themselves beautifully to the color mixing and muting that give my fine art pieces a more painterly effect.

In Russia, I had already developed my artistic language through the medium of etching, and I had graduated with a final portfolio of scenes from a trip to Prague. But I was determined that silk painting would provide me with the same detail that I could achieve with etchings. Because I was working in relative isolation, I invented many techniques to achieve my results.

Driven to expand the possibilities of silk painting, I took the art far beyond the creation of colorful floral scarves and decorative motifs for clothing and textile design, and I am now challenging myself by doing nude figures and portraiture. However, my favorite subjects are still architecture in landscape settings, and reflections in water and glass.

I am proud to be part of the worldwide renaissance of silk painters whose work in the last thirty years has brought international recognition to silk painting as a medium for fine art expression.

Each chapter of *Silk Diary* ends with a special section explaining the techniques I use to create my paintings. For those silk painters who would like to use this text as a study guide for learning how I paint on silk, I have provided a list of the techniques and their location in the book.

Illustrations & Technique Summary

1 Suzdal

My friend Julia was on the telephone, pitching me one of her crazy, last-minute schemes at the speed of light: if I could pack my camping gear, sketchbooks, and paints in one hour—and get my mother's blessing—I could be on the train to the monastery town of Suzdal, one of Russia's historical treasures. A whole gang of us, boys and girls, would sleep in the forest nearby.

Julia was one of the wildest of my school friends. Round and soft and huggable, with the milky-white skin and blue eyes of a Rubens angel, she wore her curly, red-gold hair in a long braid down to her waist. Often dressed in mismatching bohemian outfits like her artist mother, Julia favored childish woolen mittens and red rubber boots, wearing them just to thumb her nose at fashion and the world in general.

Sofia had raised Julia alone since she was a baby. She had no desire to stifle her daughter's flamboyant self-expression and good-natured enthusiasm for life, even though my irrepressible friend would take off for Kiev or Leningrad at a moment's notice, calling Sofia from a relative's apartment only after she had arrived. The year was 1976, and we were both students at a very unusual and forward-thinking art school—the most prestigious in Moscow—and at fourteen, we had already experienced much more freedom than other children our age.

I had never been to Suzdal and was very excited. Phoning my mother at the chemical research lab where she worked, I told her it was an art school activity—stretching the truth to ensure her permission.

Fifteen of us met at the train station. After a four-hour trip into the rolling hills northeast of Moscow, we changed to a bus in the city of Vladimir, and took it to Suzdal. The little town looked as if it hadn't changed since the twelfth century, when it had briefly surpassed Kiev as Russia's most important city; and we arrived at the peak of an incandescent golden-pink sunset that set aglow the cupolas and bell towers of its ancient churches. Surrounded by man-made earthworks that had been built for protection, Suzdal contained over three hundred churches and five empty monasteries.

As we walked through the town of wooden cottages and well-tended gardens, we crossed several brilliantly-green water meadows. These soggy marshes, laced with lazily meandering streams, were decorated at every turn with wildflowers and occasional cows, and we could see at least ten churches on the horizon from wherever we stood. Everyone was stunned into silence by the beauty and peaceful aura of these ancient stone buildings. Suzdal was like nothing we had ever seen before.

Sharing swigs of strong tea with us from his thermos bottle, a fellow traveler on the train had explained to us that the only forest anywhere near Suzdal was next to a little village called Kideksha. If we followed the Nerl River on an old footpath for about ten miles past Suzdal, we wouldn't get lost.

Though it was a long walk, the night was glorious and clear, and our footsteps were guided by the full moon. We sang our favorite melodies from the contemporary crop of popular Russian poet-guitarists as we walked along, happy to be having an adventure and seeing such rare beauty.

Walking into the little village of Kideksha, we stumbled upon the old monastery at its center. The cluster of moss-covered, eleventh-century churches and outbuildings, surrounded by a low stone wall, was in ruins and completely abandoned.We started hugging the buildings and feeling their cool, moonlit walls against our faces. Something outside our normal, ordinary lives as Soviet students was touching us, and many of the girls' faces were streaked with tears of joy. None of us remained outside the spell of those silent, serene buildings on the banks of the Nerl.

We found the little forest by the cemetery of the monastery and put up our tents. As I lay in my sleeping bag in Julia's tent, I was too excited to sleep. I remembered my grandmother telling stories about the *yurodivui*. These were Russia's holy wild people, completely illiterate and often retarded. They wandered about, carrying on long, rambling conversations with God and the Holy Mother, and people thought that their primitive purity gave them a direct connection to the saints.

The homeless *yurodivui* gathered together in poor encampments, and as the stories go, the founders of the early Russian Orthodox Church built their churches at these places because they believed that the simple-minded ecstatics felt the holy energy of God there. Maybe the stories are right, because we were all moved by the special beauty and energy of this peaceful place.

Early the next morning, in typical Julia style, she and I left our encampment without telling anyone. Too full of anticipation to wait for our companions, we wanted to get going, to paint, and to see everything. After hitching a ride with a tour bus on its way to Suzdal, we went though dozens of churches and museums and just wandered around, sketching whenever we felt like it.

Later in the day, we hitchhiked a ride out to Pokrava-on-the-Nerl to see the Church of the Intercession, which was famous for its unusual proportions: a tall white square with walls leaning slightly inward, its single white tower like a holy candle. In the spring, the Nerl overflows and the church becomes an island in the river. But this was early autumn, and the trees were the colors of fire: orange, yellow, and red.

We painted the church as if nothing else in the world existed. Splashes of rain from a sudden shower enhanced our work, adding shimmer and movement to the reflections of the white tower in the river.

The day was pure magic. It was the first time in my life I really understood beauty, and I was utterly submerged in it. It was wonderful enough to be insanely happy, but to have a friend like Julia to share this profound experience—someone who was excited about everything with the same wild and intense energy—that was even better.

It started raining very hard and a cold wind came up, bringing us back to reality. We couldn't find a ride back to Kideksha, and trudging along for several miles, shivering in the rain, we started feeling very guilty that we had deserted our friends. No doubt they were worried sick about us.

Beside the muddy road, we found a huge pile of potatoes. We knew it might be weeks before the local *kolhoz* got around to collecting them, and half would be wasted anyway. Since my parents had taught me to think of gleaning from the fields not as stealing, but as helping to save what would probably be spoiled, we collected as many potatoes as we could carry in our backpacks, and hunched our shoulders against the wind. This time there were neither songs nor moonlight to keep

us going, and as we crept, tired and wet, by the fog-shrouded monastery gravestones, we hoped that the little red light we saw in the forest was the campfire.

It was indeed the camp, but no one was there: our friends were out looking for us. So we built up the fire and started boiling the potatoes. Finally, giving us up as lost, they returned, and as they hungrily demolished the potato soup, they forgave us for abandoning them.

In the morning, we woke up in sleeping bags so rain-soaked you could squeeze puddles of water from them, and a few of us had developed bad coughs and were sneezing. So the boys decided it was the perfect time to drink some vodka, for its "healing properties." I had never tried it, but I was so cold and wet that they probably could have convinced me to drink kerosene, as long as it turned up the temperature.

Somehow, the boys had gotten their hands on several bottles of cheap vodka, and we passed them around, shivering in our soggy sleeping bags. Soon the burning liquid produced the right effect, and we became wild artists again. The sun came out and drew us back to the monastery, where we continued drawing and painting from our new drunken perspective.

Gradually, as the alcohol wore off, we all took different buses back to Suzdal and wandered around the town. Since we had run out of money and were quite hungry, we lived on apples we had scavenged from orchards earlier that day.

Julia and I were so happy about what we had seen and felt. We would be returning home with piles of sketches and water colors, completely in our element as artists.

This trip to Suzdal will always stand out in my memory as my first taste of "the artist's life," and was a model of sorts for all my sketching and painting trips to come: an unlikely combination of deep spiritual connection, brilliant creativity, and hilarious adventures. All my paintings of Suzdal reflect my feelings about the subtle beauty of Russia and the mystical power of this special place—the sense of Russia's history as it is held in ancient stone churches and monasteries. I have been back many times since then, and Suzdal has almost always filled me with a sense of peace and comfort—with a healing energy. Whenever I enter the environs of Suzdal, all the worries and stresses of my life disappear, and I feel full of inspiration and in love with simply being alive.

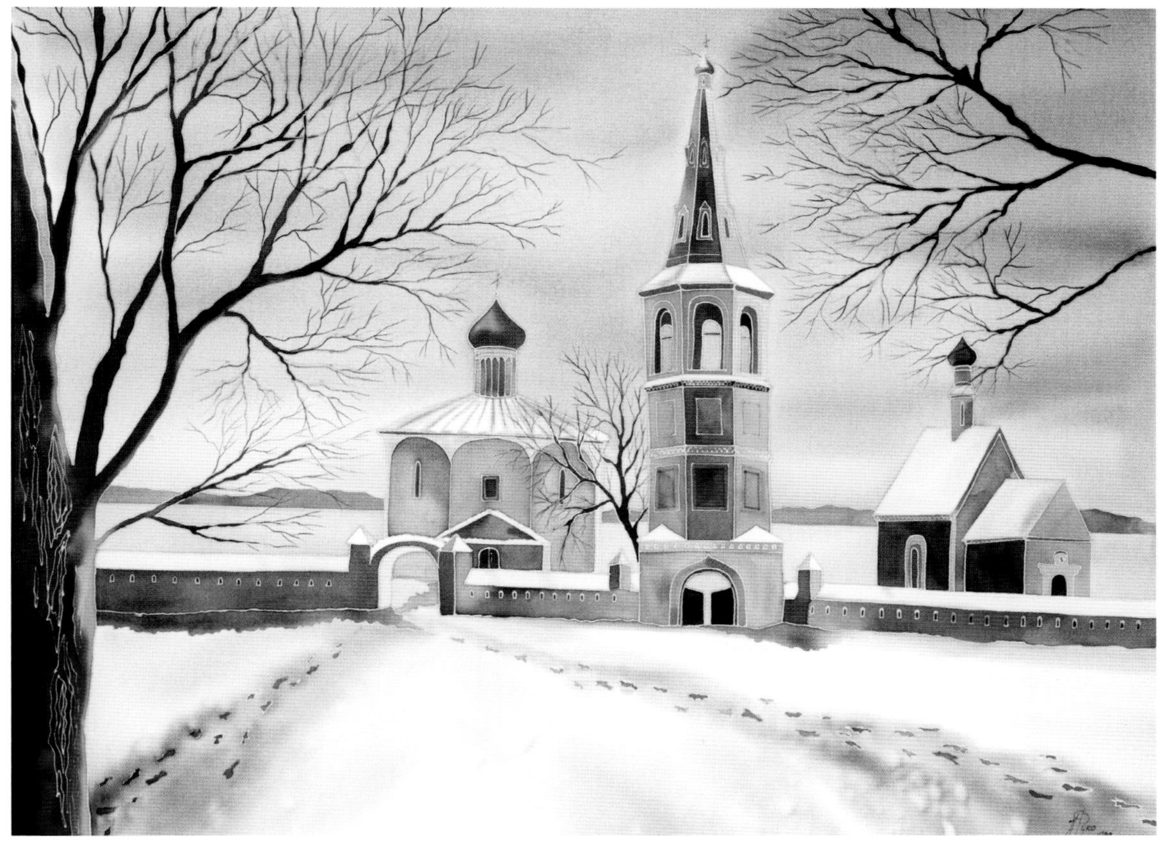

Kideksha on the River Nerl

Technique

During my travels, I take hundreds of photographs to capture images of the places and scenes I want to paint. But before I take the picture, I use the frame of my viewfinder to compose the painting, setting its basic elements from the outset.

The details of buildings or other landscape elements are often unreadable on a photograph, although colors are recorded fairly accurately. So a few well-executed sketches, drawn at the same time as I take the photographs, always help me to remember all the sharp details that my eye can see. I often follow the compositional rule of using three planes of view in my paintings, with the sharper, brighter details in the plane closest to the viewer, and softer colors and fewer details as the planes recede into the distance.

Many students ask me how I decide which details to leave in and which to remove. I look at the total composition of my final sketch, removing and adding the ones that create the best balance. Often I move a building or a tree to another part of the painting in order to find this balance.

The work of photographing and sketching at the beginning of the process is necessary to create a painting that looks natural and effortless. In "Kideksha on the River Nerl," I eliminated many of the buildings in my photograph to give the painting a sense of serenity. And I added the footprints in the snow to lead the viewer's eye through the stone archway to the buildings beyond.

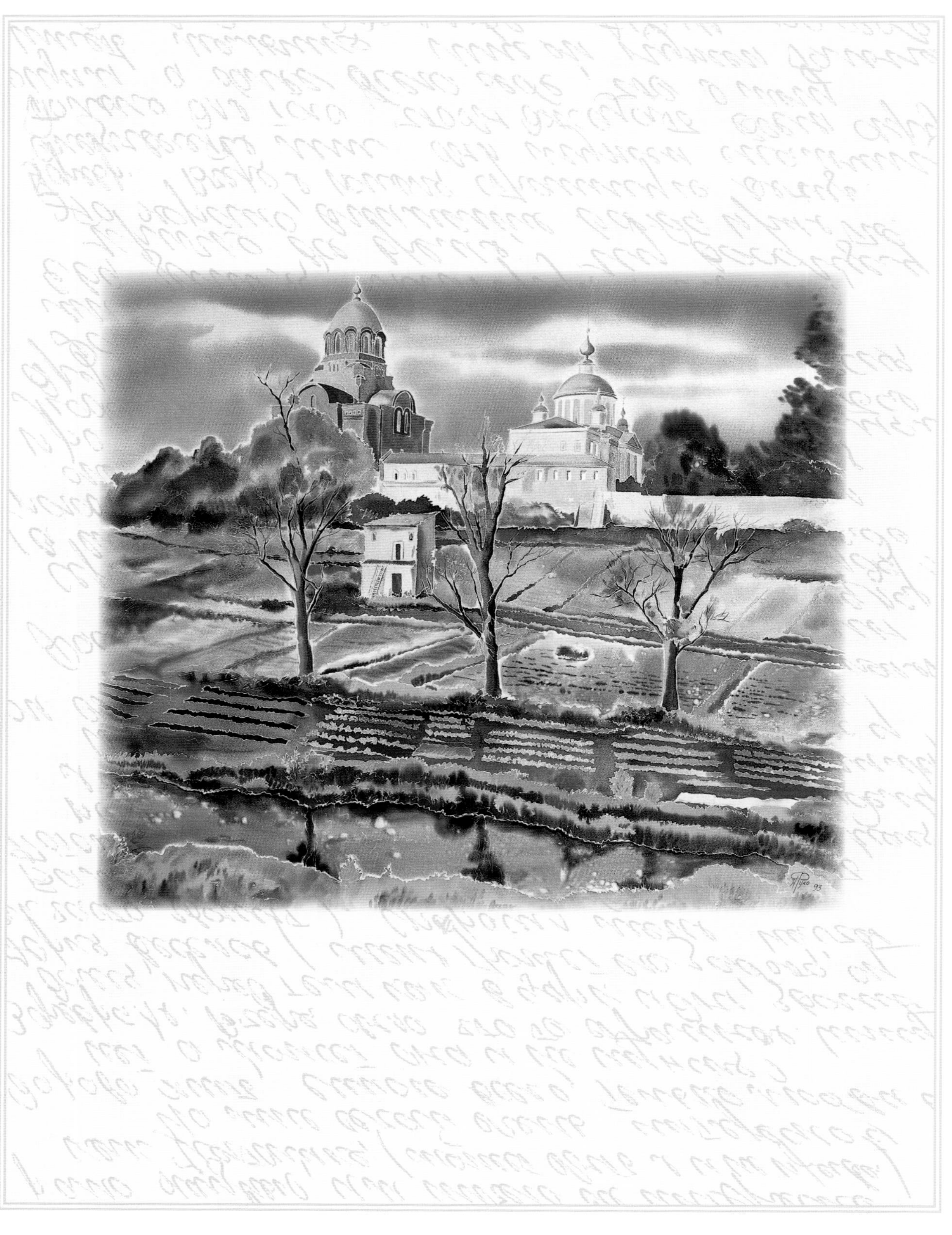

2 Vasin

Children's Art School Number One was one of the best in all of Moscow, and once I had announced my desire to be an artist, my family had fought to get me in. On my second attempt to pass the exam, at age fourteen, I had been accepted, and soon Julia and I had become good friends. In the Soviet system, children began art training at age five, so I was considered a late starter. Perhaps that was why I worked twice as hard as everyone else to make sure I succeeded.

To a great extent, the charismatic personality of our favorite teacher, Vasin, gave our art school its reputation for being unusual and innovative. For some reason it was also less hampered by political restrictions and Party meddling than the other specialized high schools.

Vasin was unusual by any standards. Everybody loved this talented, fascinating man, with his long golden hair and piercing blue eyes. But at thirty, he was already bitter and broken, because his life was one of unfulfilled expectations. He would talk to us about things that nobody, even our parents, would dare discuss. My parents didn't agree with the system and let me know it by making occasional pointed comments about the government, but Vasin was downright defiant. He was completely anti-Soviet, raging against all of the government's faults and corruption, and told us about Solzhenitsyn and the prison camps.

The key element in his philosophy of life was the ancient Greek idea of catharsis. Aristotle had written about cleansing the soul by witnessing suffering—perhaps a death—and deeply experiencing that suffering along with the victim.

Being told about these things at the age of fourteen was overwhelming. In many ways, we were just typical teenagers, coming to school and chattering about our friends or the blue jeans we had just managed to find. But being exposed to all this secret knowledge made us feel like a chosen group of special insiders. Of course, we didn't discuss what Vasin told us with our parents or anyone else.

Each summer, we spent one month away from school, taking field trips and painting outdoors. During this plenary session, as it was called, students would go to the Red Square, the zoo, or a monastery to sketch and paint. One year, Vasin decided he would take the whole class to his *dacha*.

A typical Russian family owns or rents a retreat place, or dacha, which they visit as often as possible during the warm summer months. These range from palatial mansions for the privileged to simple wooden cabins or gardening sheds with a small plot of vegetables—a train ride away from the crumbling, concrete high rise apartment houses surrounding Moscow.

The school director, Lapin, grilled Vasin about his plan. It was impossible, the director stammered; Vasin would never manage it: one adult with fifteen unruly adolescents was a formula for mayhem. But Vasin's charisma and brilliance made him the favorite of everyone, even the director. It was why he managed to be so outspoken without being betrayed to Party authorities. Finally, Lapin relented, and Vasin met our class at his dacha in the Podolsk farmlands.

I arrived three or four days late, because I had been taking extra classes at the architectural school, and had several exams to complete. My parents drove me to the village of Lipovtsy, and as we arrived, we passed Vasin on his battered bicycle. I was shocked to see that he had cut off his beautiful golden hair, shaved his head, and wore a long purple velvet robe. My parents were very young and naive, and usually assumed everything was going well at my school. So they just dropped me off, completely ignoring Vasin's weird appearance.

The next day, I started passing out art materials and straightening the sleeping areas, like the class monitor I was during the regular school year. But during the next few days, I slowly began to understand that this was going to be nothing like a regular plenary session, with organized outdoor drawing trips. Vasin took absolutely no responsibility for anything we did, and was even unconcerned about whether or not we had anything to eat or drink. One of us was assigned to bring to him a cup of black tea every morning, which he seemed to subsist on. We had no idea that he was fortifying it with vodka.

After a few days, we began to get really hungry. Since all of us were fairly spoiled city kids, we had no idea how to cook. We tried to make macaroni and cheese, but it stuck to the pot and burned. Fortunately, the boys of the village, who laughed at us as we painted near their homes, brought us cottage cheese, milk, and vegetables from their gardens once they realized we were starving. Luckily, too, we stayed relatively clean; a river flowed nearby, and we swam and bathed there after our outdoor drawing sessions.

Although he had almost totally abandoned responsibility for his little group, Vasin retained some concept of making us into his version of "real" human beings, and in the evenings, we were all expected to come together in the large room, where Vasin would tell us what he thought of us.

"Natasha," he would begin, when it was my turn in the spotlight, "you have such a big ego, but no talent to go with it. You ruined three sheets of my special water color paper from France. Believe me, it's very expensive and not for the likes of you."

"And you, Sonya," he continued, "all you're interested in is flirting with the boys and showing off your excellent legs. You are wasting my time by even being here..."

Of course, he was very perceptive, and much of what he said was true. He felt that we had to experience catharsis by being completely stripped of our defenses and reduced to nothing. But being exposed like that in front of each other left many of us in tears—our faces burning from shame and embarrassment. We would huddle together on our beds past midnight, drinking valerian tea for our nerves, and analyzing what Vasin had said about us.

Then there was Vasin's Theory of Drinking Vodka, a self-contained philosophical treatise about becoming real artists with the help of the bottle. He told us we must completely wipe out the distractions of everyday life and focus intensely on the painting we were working on. Without vodka, the subtleties of light and shade and color—our means to express feelings and emotions—would be hidden from us. We would just be good technicians. Although I didn't start drinking then, his words came back to me later at the Moscow Art Institute, when everyone around me was drinking like a fish. Then I remembered Vasin's compelling explanations of the need for vodka, and started to toss down shots like my friends.

Vasin's bitterness arose from his truncated career. He had been a brilliant cartoonist, but his political jibes at the government had become too strong for the authorities, and he had been interrogated and sent to prison for a few years to be "rehabilitated." From an artistic standpoint, however, his work was so exceptional that in classes earlier that spring, we had been given his cartoons so we could study his style. But the images and text had been chopped into little pieces by the education censors so we couldn't read their political content! Since Vasin needed to focus his prodigious energy somewhere and couldn't develop his life as he had envisioned it, our little group became his obsession.

I was the first one to be sent back to Moscow before the session ended. My efforts to keep everyone organized and maintain some semblance of a daily routine began to irritate Vasin. Apparently, I wasn't transforming into a completely free spirit fast enough. When I showed up back in Moscow at the regular art practices, the director of the school pulled me out of the room and hustled me down to his office.

I couldn't possibly explain to Lapin what was going on at the dacha in Lipovtsy. By this time, Vasin had become sexually involved with one of the female students, a girl fifteen years younger than him. Though he later married her and they stayed together for many years, there was going to be a scandal if anyone found out at that point. A few days later, Vasin banished another set of students, one of whom told her mother about his vodka theory. Then the whole thing unraveled: Vasin was convicted in court of consorting with a student, and thrown out of the school.

All of the teachers tried to get us to tell them what we had done to Vasin. They loved him, and were mortified that he had been thrown out. And for many years afterward, we continued to visit our mentor. After he married his ex-student, Irina, he started drinking very heavily, until he was eventually consumed by his alcoholism. Though his life was ruined, he had profoundly affected us and changed us irrevocably. He had made us feel exceptional, and provided another step in the pathway I was creating for myself, away from the stable lifestyle of my family of chemists and engineers.

Vasin's theories of art were in line with his philosophy of life: we must eliminate our ordinary ideas to become real artists. At first, no one could understand why he told us that when painting green, we should throw the green tubes of paint out of our painting kits.

"If you want your paintings to look like the work of a complete amateur," he would shout, "just keep using Thalo green! You must feel for the colors in your bones. Strain your eyes to see them!"

I took all his admonitions seriously, and spent the rest of that summer mixing every one of the colors I used. That's how I learned to see colors as they actually appeared, and not limited by my concept of them.

Technique

When I paint on silk, I still remember Vasin's shouts of advice, and I mix every color that I apply. I use small squares of white ceramic tile as palettes for mixing brushes full of color, which allows me to see it clearly before I apply it to the silk. This way, I avoid disastrous applications of unmodulated dye.

In order to work as freely as I do, without recipes or formulas, a silk painter must be thoroughly grounded in a clear understanding of color mixing, and not be seduced by the hundreds of brilliant colors available from the companies that sell silk dyes. Since these dyes are chemicals and not pure light, however, the theory must be modified to account for this difference. For instance, in pure color theory, equal amounts of yellow and purple—opposites on the color wheel—will make a neutral gray, while in fact, most yellow and purple dye combinations will yield a very useful range of olive greens.

In the painting "Village Life," created many years after my summer with Vasin, the colors I used give the feeling of many water color sketches I executed under his tutelage. Even though the photograph I worked from shows a green table, a green plant in the window, and a green meadow and trees outside the window, there is very little actual green in the painting, because I have diluted and muddied, or darkened and saturated, all the colors with generous additions of brown, blue, and black. I also make constant use of the little leftover cups of "mud colors"—familiar to silk painters—to mute out the brilliant hues that are contained in the dye bottles.

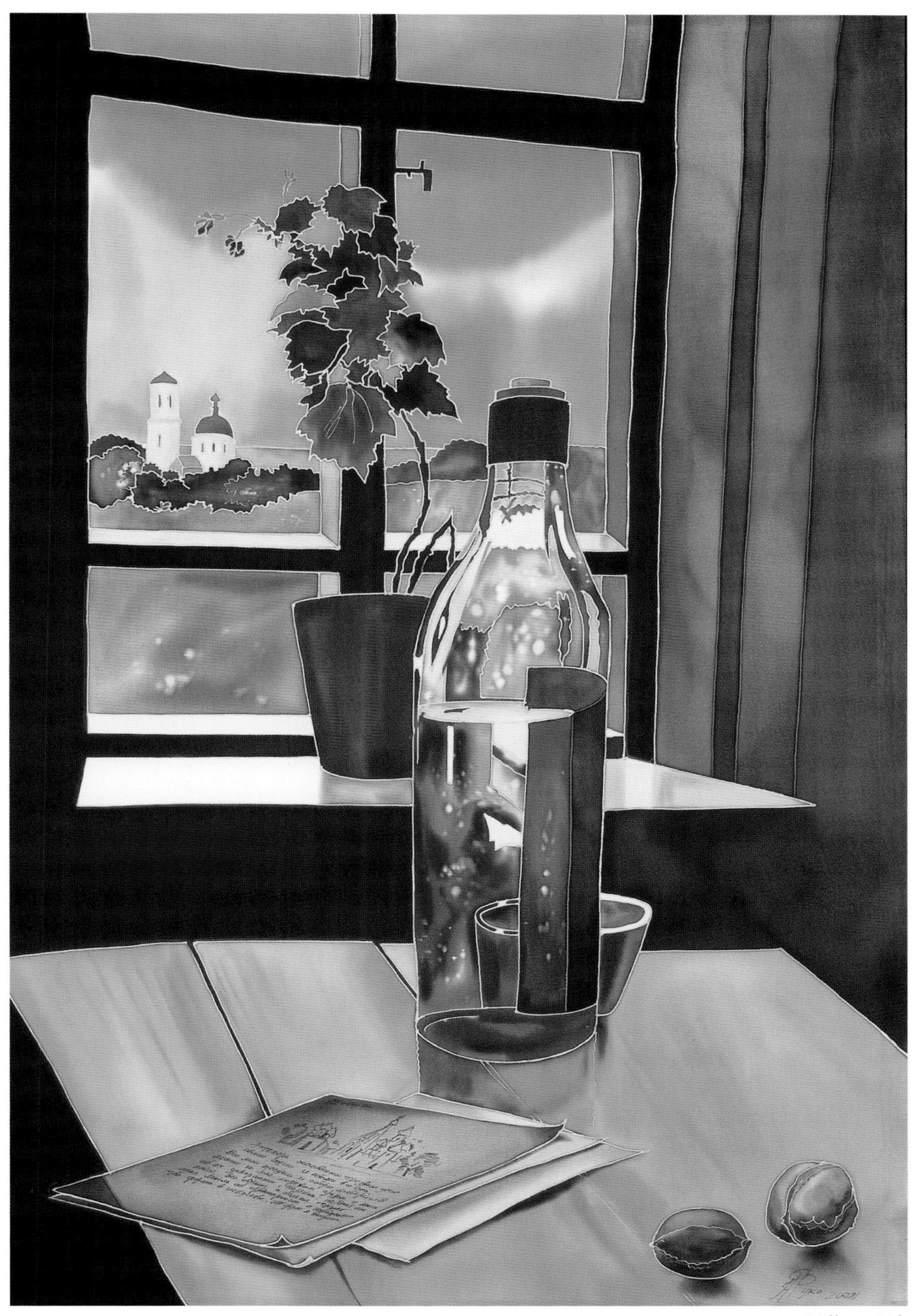

Village Life

Мне [illegible] всё дело рисовать [illegible]
все более и более заинтересовываюсь [illegible]
[illegible] интересная жизнь. А [illegible]
мне совершенно не нужно. Первый [illegible]
это [illegible]
[illegible]

[illegible] февр.
[illegible] Вот
что добрые, вот что я люблю! [illegible]
[illegible]
У нас с собой [illegible]
Приехала я в 5, а в 5.15 приехала Надя
потом Саша [illegible] с цветами, а
через час Ольга. Мы интересно [illegible]
в [illegible] с Ольгой [illegible]
[illegible]
Хочу [illegible] с [illegible]
и поговорить [illegible] было интересно.
Сегодня [illegible]
февраля Сегодня у [illegible] интересный [illegible]
[illegible]
мне не хватает времени. [illegible]
в школе, там у нас [illegible] очень интерес[illegible]

3 The Apple Orchard

I will never forget the autumn I discovered Sukhanovo. It was the year after our trip to Suzdal. This tiny Russian village, nestled in forests and orchards about an hour's train ride from Moscow, had been gradually transformed over the years into a retirement community for architects. I had come upon it by chance when I happened to get off the train there one day after school. After that, I would occasionally skip classes and, without telling anybody, would go to Sukhanovo for the whole day and wander through its jumbled maze of streets. Each turn of the road revealed clusters of little houses with gardens, and orchards full of apple trees. In October, they always burned the autumn leaves, and the smell, with a smoky haze, filled the air. To this day, when I smell burning leaves in autumn, I am immediately back in Sukhanovo.

At the north end of the village, retired architects had indulged their most cherished building fantasies, and a whole collection of residences—replicating dozens of architectural syles—reflected dramatically in the deep, cool waters of several lakes. A Greek temple portico stood next to a miniature Russian tsar's palace or an English Tudor mansion. It was a treasure trove of inspiration for sketching and painting.

But what particularly drew me back to Sukhanovo time and again was a dead apple orchard. Though a live apple orchard was maintained right next to it, I would always visit the dead trees first—old grandmothers with twisted, gnarly limbs like arthritic hands. I'm not sure why. Perhaps it was the beauty of the branches silhouetted against the smoky haze. The trees always reminded me of Van Gogh's trees with hands—they looked like people screaming in anguish. I was never satisfied with my paintings of them and tried several times over to capture the subtle appeal of the dead orchard.

One day, I went there with my painting materials in hand, and stood, shocked. The dead orchard had been completely cut to the ground. There was nothing left—just some pieces of trees here and there like dismembered arms and legs. It was horrible, and I felt like I had lost somebody, like a person had died. I was stunned. How could something so precious to me just disappear? My painting, "The Apple Orchard," expresses my feelings about this place of beauty and about death and the uncertainty of the future.

When my life-long friend, Misha, saw the painting, he was inspired to write a poem about paradise lost, and the journey of the soul.

The apple orchard destroyed
Those poor black branches
They are like a reproach to us
There are many apples in the orchard
Still lying on the ground
Like a rug which is alive
I am stepping on them
As on open wounds
And here's a person in my hand
Like a shining but cold note
You can't warm it up
There's more, tens, hundreds

The steps of the ladder of salvation
Are unreachable
Our way to simplicity is bitter
Our birth a flight, falling, rotten
It was a lesson, the soul falling
The barefoot youth rustles dead leaves
As she walks

Misha's perspective was totally novel to me, as I didn't have any of these ideas in mind when I painted the image. For the first time, I realized that any piece of art—any sincere and truthful art—is only a mirror. What the viewer sees when he looks at it is colored by his own thoughts. So by looking at a painting, you can see what's inside of you, and what is important to you.

This painting marked a turning point in my development as an artist. I now felt that it absolutely did not matter what I wanted to say in my work: what mattered was what the viewer saw in the mirror of the painting. And I realized that it wasn't my job to figure out the significance of any of the paintings; it was simply my job to paint them. This insight freed me up to focus on just becoming a good painter. Everything else would take care of itself.

The Apple Orchard

Technique

One of my teachers at the Art Institute would give us an exercise. She would say a word that denoted an emotion or an idea—like mystery, love, or betrayal. Thinking of the painting as expressing just that one word, we would use color and line to capture its power. In "The Apple Orchard," I use color to paint autumn as death.

In the orchard of clumsily sawed-off trunks, a ladder goes up into the poisonous, mustard-colored sky, obscured by a dirty grayish cloud. Having painted the tree trunks in dark brown and black, I needed a contrasting color for the trees in the background, and rendered them in an eerie combination of gray and blood red. The two girls seem trapped in a fog that creeps deathlike across the foreground. And even the golden apples do not look alive, since they reflect the polluted gold of the sky. No one has chosen this painting to hang on their walls. It's just too unsettling.

4 St. Petersburg

The windows of the chilly, drab classroom of the Moscow Art Institute looked out onto an eighteenth century German cemetery in an ugly neighborhood. A few blocks away, the notorious Lefortovo prison sat hulking over endless rows of workers' apartments.

Our art classes at the Institute were matched by an equal number of boring lectures on Marxist-Leninist theory. I stayed awake through the endless political droning by secretively sketching the elaborately carved headstones of the old cemetery in the margins of my notebook.

Some of the Institute's art classes were extremely difficult—modeled on dusty nineteenth century principles of discipline and repetition—while others were creative and full of color and experimentation. But in between all the classes and exams, I was able to have fun doing what I loved the most—traveling. Although trips abroad were next to impossible in those days, travel inside the Soviet Union was very easy. And, as my parents gave me a lot of freedom, I was able to go by myself or with friends quite often.

My first trip to what was then Leningrad—a six hour train trip—was during my first fall semester at the Art Institute. I was accompanied by two school mates, one of whom had an aunt in the city center with whom we could stay.

Train rides in the Soviet Union had their own special feel and traditions. We always went at night, so as not to waste precious daytime hours getting to our destination. The train attendants would roll a cart with a big brass samovar down the corridor, offering steaming glasses of tea in cut-work metallic holders. Long conversations with fellow travelers in the six-person compartments helped pass the hours: perhaps it was the strong tea that made Russians talk to complete strangers on train rides. Or perhaps it was the knowledge that we would never see each other again. Since we never knew who might be reporting on us, we rarely shared details of our personal lives or feelings with someone we saw every day, such as a co-worker.

There were some older folks in our compartment one evening who looked like typical Soviet citizens, wrapped securely in their dull-colored wool coats and worn fur hats, carrying canvas bags loaded with traveling goods. But as soon as they learned we were art students, they told us they were artists, too—but secret ones—and gave us an address in St. Petersburg where we could visit them.

These were the first underground artists we had ever met. They had never been accepted into the Party-dominated Artists Union, either because of their politics or the content of their paintings. Though they looked really worn down, they also had an air of romance and bohemian chic. With the eagerness of youth, we were ready for an adventure, and for some reason, the artists seemed to trust us. Perhaps it was our obvious innocence.

We decided to visit our new friends, and followed their directions to an old, run-down section of St. Petersburg. The wooden door of Number 45 had only a few traces of paint left on its cracked and weather-beaten planks. Inside, every available wall space was covered with drawings, etchings, and oil paintings, but there wasn't a single worker or peasant with bulging muscles standing triumphantly by his grain thresher or iron smelter—in the government-approved Social Realism style. These artists were inspired by the pre-Revolutionary Cubism of Kandinsky and Klee, and the fantastic imagery of Chagall.

By the end of the day, we had visited four apartments filled with these indefatigable old artists and their illegal exhibitions. Each one handed us off to the next with an address scribbled on a slip of paper. We were enthralled. This was our first taste of the real life of artists—an experience that had not been programmed into our official education.

That visit to the clandestine exhibits of the underground artists colored the way I viewed St. Petersburg. It was where real art flourished, even if it was behind locked doors and hung on moldy walls. I began to take regular trips to the city by myself, at least four times a year.

I established my own special routine for these trips. Taking the midnight train, I would ride for the six hours half-asleep, lulled by the rhythmic sound of the wheels on the tracks. Then instead of going directly to the apartment of some university friends of my mother, where I would be staying for a few days, I would stuff my bags into a locker at the train station and begin to prowl the misty, fog-shrouded streets of St. Petersburg, which were almost totally empty of people. Only a few lights pierced the post-dawn gloom, emphasizing the city's tragic, deeply haunting beauty.

The well-heeled tourists who now swarm off the luxury cruise ships docking at St. Petersburg in the summer

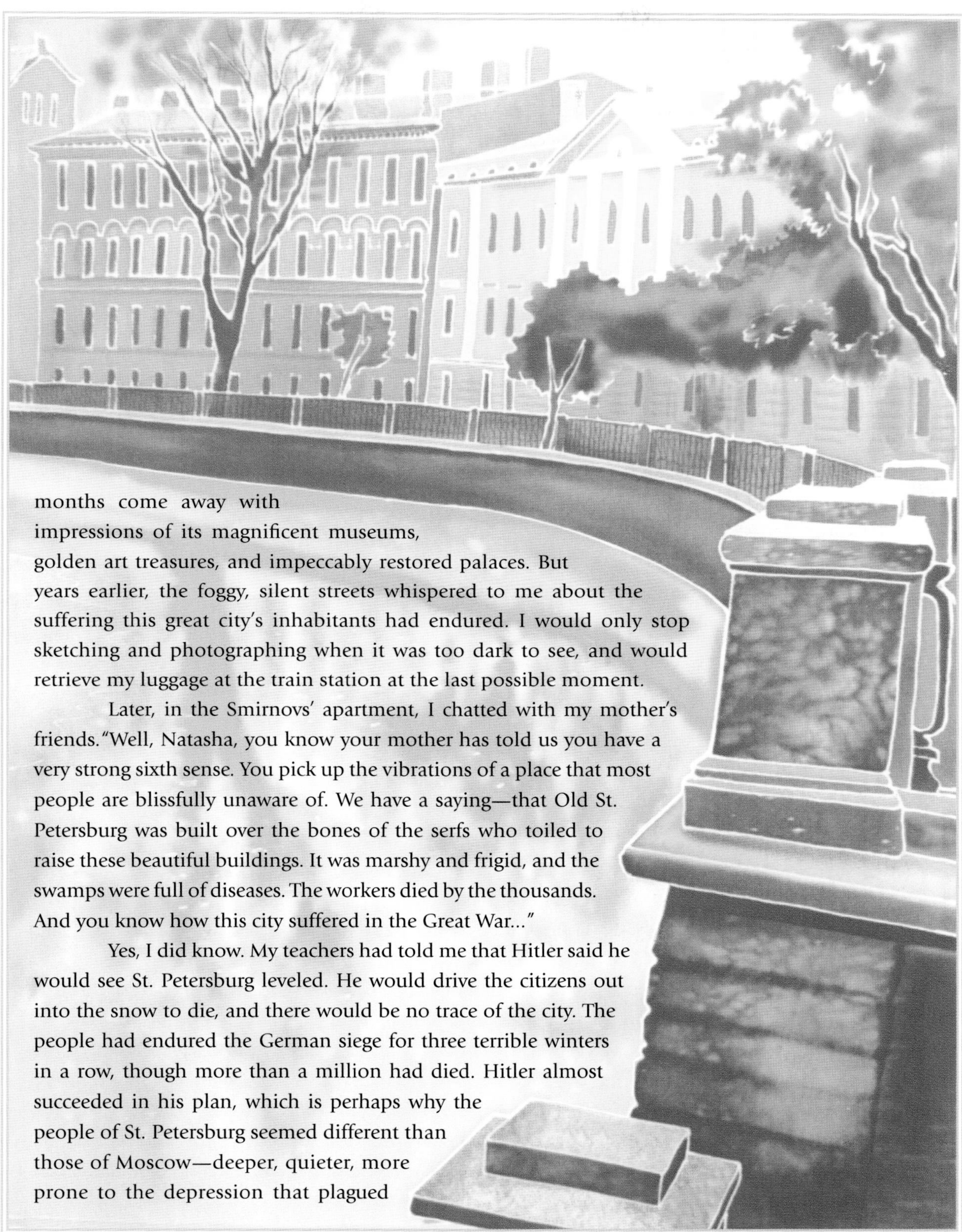

months come away with impressions of its magnificent museums, golden art treasures, and impeccably restored palaces. But years earlier, the foggy, silent streets whispered to me about the suffering this great city's inhabitants had endured. I would only stop sketching and photographing when it was too dark to see, and would retrieve my luggage at the train station at the last possible moment.

Later, in the Smirnovs' apartment, I chatted with my mother's friends. "Well, Natasha, you know your mother has told us you have a very strong sixth sense. You pick up the vibrations of a place that most people are blissfully unaware of. We have a saying—that Old St. Petersburg was built over the bones of the serfs who toiled to raise these beautiful buildings. It was marshy and frigid, and the swamps were full of diseases. The workers died by the thousands. And you know how this city suffered in the Great War..."

Yes, I did know. My teachers had told me that Hitler said he would see St. Petersburg leveled. He would drive the citizens out into the snow to die, and there would be no trace of the city. The people had endured the German siege for three terrible winters in a row, though more than a million had died. Hitler almost succeeded in his plan, which is perhaps why the people of St. Petersburg seemed different than those of Moscow—deeper, quieter, more prone to the depression that plagued our long winters.

But I also experienced the bright magnificence and golden beauty of St. Petersburg, just like any other tourist. And I always returned from my sketching trips full of inspiration and ideas for paintings.

My favorite places were the grand parks where the tsars and tsarinas had built their summer residences. Over the years, they had erected palaces in the countryside surrounding this elegant, architecturally brilliant city—the creation of Peter the Great as his window onto Europe, and Western philosophy and fashion. The names of the palaces roll off my tongue like pearls on a necklace: Pavlovsk, Pushkin, Oranienbaum, Gatchina. In fact, St. Petersburg has been called the "Venice of the North" because of the magnificent beauty of its buildings, and its many canals, with their myriad possibilities for creating great reflections.

I had always been fascinated with painting water and reflections, a passion that still inspires my work now. Perhaps that was why I was so happy sketching and drawing in St. Petersburg.

Technique

During these student days, I developed the methods and practices which I still use to create my paintings. First, I took tons of photographs with the camera my parents had given me for my seventeenth birthday. It was my most treasured possession, and I was never without it.

I would return to my cramped little bedroom in our Moscow apartment—half of which was piled to the ceiling with my art supplies and paintings. I would spread out all the photographs I had taken of a particular image, and tack them to the wall, along with all the pen and ink and watercolor sketches I had done at the same site. I would use them to make a study for the painting. Often, too, I took elements from several different photos and sketches and combined them in one painting. All the dry, academic classes I had taken at the Institute on perspective and architecture bore fruit, and gave me the fundamental tools I needed to create interesting, realistic paintings. I never merely copied from the photos.

It was during these artistic journeys to St. Petersburg that I began to create layers in my paintings by depicting reflections on glass. Later, in the silk painting "Teahouse at Oranienbaum," I created another of these paintings with multiple layers. I had taken my photograph outside the window of a narrow wing of the teahouse, and the nude statue at the left of the painting is a reflection on the window I looked through. That statue was actually behind me, whereas the statue on the black pedestal was inside the teahouse, and the one in the center of the painting was on the far side of the building—outside the window on the far wall. If you look carefully at the top of the painting, you will see an indication of my hand on the left side, and a gray shape in the center, which represents the reflection of my hair in the window as I take the photograph.

I find these layers of a painting in reflections to be most intriguing, and I continue to paint them. My poet friend, Misha, tells me that this is one of the strongest metaphysical elements of my work.

"You say you paint reflections in water and glass just because you love them. But I think it's the way you express the multiplicity of reality. Your work has a symbolic overtone to it that hints of the seen and the unseen worlds." He adds, "Your paintings have a profound spiritual presence. But as you say, maybe it's your job to paint, and the job of crazy poets like me to interpret your paintings for you..."

Teahouse at Oranienbaum

мне интересен [illegible] [illegible]
и не в верхнем. Они [illegible]
[illegible] им ничего не интересно
[illegible] (может быть я и не права)
но мне сейчас очень интересно
[illegible] [illegible] любви
нет [illegible]
[illegible]
[illegible]
[illegible]
[illegible]
[illegible]
[illegible]
[illegible]
[illegible]
[illegible]
[illegible]
[illegible]
Достоев[illegible] [illegible]
[illegible] [illegible]
[illegible] [illegible] за собой [illegible]
(а [illegible] [illegible] обратно) [illegible]
поговорить, [illegible] у нас была [illegible]
сказать, он мне все все рассказал
про свою девочку, [illegible]
любовь. Теперь я смотрю что [illegible]
[illegible] [illegible] обязательно
[illegible] девочки. [illegible] интересная
[illegible] стала, хорошие все же
[illegible] [illegible]
[illegible] все время. [illegible]

5 Flight

Just before the 1980 Summer Olympics, all the students in Moscow were sent out of town to make room for hordes of foreign visitors. But we were never told why we had to leave, and the visitors never came.

During this time, I reluctantly took an assignment as the ceramics teacher at a Young Pioneer camp. Elated and dazed by the excitement of my first love affair, I could barely conceal my frustration at having to leave Moscow.

The camp was in the pine forests of Tuchkovo, away from the stifling heat and dust of the city. And in the endless twilight of the Russian midsummer, the evenings were softly surreal. I would lie in bed in my one-room cabin lit by a single kerosene lantern, with only mosquitoes and crickets disturbing the velvety stillness. My sole entertainment was reading the books I had brought with me: women artists, Greek architecture, Roman history. My mother's friend Katya, who worked at an elite library for the theatre, had slipped me a membership card when backs were turned.

In that library, I had discovered the lusciously immoral *Lives of the Twelve Caesars* by the Roman historian Suetonius, and had stuffed it into my knapsack with my clothes. I read about Augustus, Claudius, and Nero, poisonings and perversions, secret sexual pleasures, and a decaying empire about to collapse inwardly like over-ripe fruit. Every night, draped in my mosquito netting, I immersed myself in the lives of these long-dead characters. I wanted to live with them and experience Rome's strength and grandeur and wild abandon. Then, too, endless fantasies about my new lover, Dima, were entwined with scenes from Roman orgies as I replayed every detail of our previous spring together in the theatre of my memories.

I had been working late every evening at the art school, pushing myself to prepare for final exams, when an unusually warm spring wind blew in through the open windows of the empty classroom. I felt someone watching me and looked toward the doorway. There, slouched in a tattered army overcoat, a dark-haired art student acknowledged my gaze with a nod, an unlit cigarette dangling from a corner of his lips. But it was his eyes that pinned me to my chair. They were a deep green—cat eyes—unblinking and flecked with gold.

We became lovers a few days later. I would meet him in his cluttered studio on the fifth floor of a once-grand apartment building in the decaying old heart of the city. Drawings and photographs of nude models taped over the crumbling plaster walls were the mute witnesses to my first sexual encounters.

Dima's strong, charismatic personality had helped him survive a tour of duty in the Russian army. Most young men were brutalized by the experience, but my lover, now twenty-six, had come away with nothing worse than a sarcastic attitude and a fistful of songs for his guitar. He had set several of his own poems to music, and had a soulfully expressive voice. The pain in his lyrics spoke volumes to me; we would drink vodka together and argue about the meaning of life. Like an addict on heroin, Dima mainlined anything tragic: Dostoevsky's novels, Hamlet, untimely death, people possessed by uncontrollable desires.

I'd be happy to say that he was an incredible lover who awakened me to all the pleasures of my body. Unfortunately, though, I didn't melt at the touch of a sensually playful man until much later in life. With Dima, I was completely inexperienced, and I deferred to his needs and wishes in bed. I had no idea that my own satisfaction was even possible.

He tossed my soul around with the force of a hurricane. I would leave his studio exhausted and shaken like a rag doll, stripped of all my notions of what life should be like. My consciousness had been awakened by the adrenaline rush of his personality, and I always came back for more.

And then there was the view from his tall bay window. The Pushkin Art Museum, across

from his apartment, was my favorite place in all of Moscow, and I loved the view almost as much as I loved Dima. My lifelong fascination with windows—painting views from windows, reflections in windows—started during those spring nights overlooking the museum gardens. I stood there many times after our lovemaking, looking out on the dark grounds—enraptured, connected to life and the world.

When my mother met Dima, she immediately disliked him. What parent would want her only child to be involved with such a rebellious guy? Everything that attracted me to this unpredictable man made my mother grimace. Her idea of a suitable boyfriend for me was her friend Zoya's son Sergei, a shy accounting student—the more boring, the better. But at least Dima was giving me some experience of life, she thought. For years, I had done nothing but study and paint and sketch, and the seeds she had planted, in an attempt to get me involved in the social life of an ordinary teenager, had fallen on sterile ground.

Lying in my solitary cabin at Pioneer Camp, I would count the days before I could see Dima again. Finally, I managed to arrange a day off from teaching, telling no one about my plans. After the three-hour train ride back to Moscow, I emerged from the Metro station into a downpour. But before turning left toward Dima's studio on Marx-Engels Street, I stopped at the iron gates of the Pushkin Art Museum. Maybe I should visit the museum first, I thought. Although I was aching to be with him, I knew my excitement would heighten the beauty of my favorite art treasures.

I went straight to the antiquities wing. The brightly-lit rooms of Greek statues were usually quiet, but that day they were completely deserted. And the guard, who was routinely posted on a little antique chair at the entrance to the Roman Hall, was off having tea with her cronies. I tiptoed in, not wanting to break the stillness.

The high ceiling of the room was an arc of emerald green glass, while the walls were painted a rich olive. With the rain and clouds obscuring the sun, the room was bathed in a luminous green aura. I felt like I was inside an aquarium—only the water was outside, drumming steadily on the glass ceiling.

In the center of the room, on an elaborately gilded table, stood a graceful bronze sculpture of Winged Nike, the Roman Goddess of Victory. She was balancing on one toe on a large bronze ball, and surrounded by two-dozen Roman heads looking outward: realistic marble portraits of the emperors. As I began to circle slowly around the table, their marble eyes followed me, a masterful trick the Alexandrian sculptors had created. Marble can reflect the smallest amount of daylight, and the smooth stone flesh glowed with life in the surreal, green-tinged room.

Hypnotically, I circled and circled, drunk on art, and on my crazy love. I was locked into this ring of staring eyes while the rain drummed relentlessly. Around and around I went; I felt weightless, my feet no longer touching the polished wood floor. What was happening? Then I floated up to the ceiling and looked down, watching myself circling the table. I soared over Moscow—just under the rain clouds—and over all my favorite streets, the golden-domed churches, the crumbling mansions.

I had no sense of directing my flying or of having a body. I was at one with the act of flying itself, a seamless feeling with no ending or beginning. It was an exultation—a rapture of weightlessness and freedom.

Suddenly, I was back beside the table of marble heads. How long had I been gone? I rushed out of the museum to Dima's studio. Our lovemaking was quick, and he seemed irritable. He didn't want to hear about my rapturous, out-of-body experience.

Over the years, I have tried to recreate that experience by putting together the same magic ingredients. I desperately wanted to float free again, but it has never happened. Sometimes I begin to paint the image, and while painting, I feel a touch of the same lightness. I have painted "Flight" many times, and in this version, you can see me floating close to the ceiling, over the bronze statue of winged Nike. Perhaps it was my soul that temporarily left my body. But how do you paint your soul?

Technique

The key element of "Flight" is the contrast of the bronze statue of Nike and the marble figures. Like snow, marble reflects the colors of objects around it, and artists often study marble to explore the subtleties of light reflections. In the large marble figure in the foreground, I have added tones of orange, fuchsia, green, and purple to the neutral gray. To make the grayish-white of marble come alive and give it roundness and depth, I also separated the gray itself into as many tones as possible. Unfortunately, premixed commercial dyes are never dark enough to give me a complete range, so I use the dye that dries at the bottom of mixing cups when I need an opaque, intense darkness.

By contrast, on the bronze statue, I used sharper jumps from light to dark to indicate its high gloss. I also intensified the reds and oranges to both emphasize the warmth of the bronze and to bring the eye back to the figure of my soul floating in the green-tinged space above.

Flight

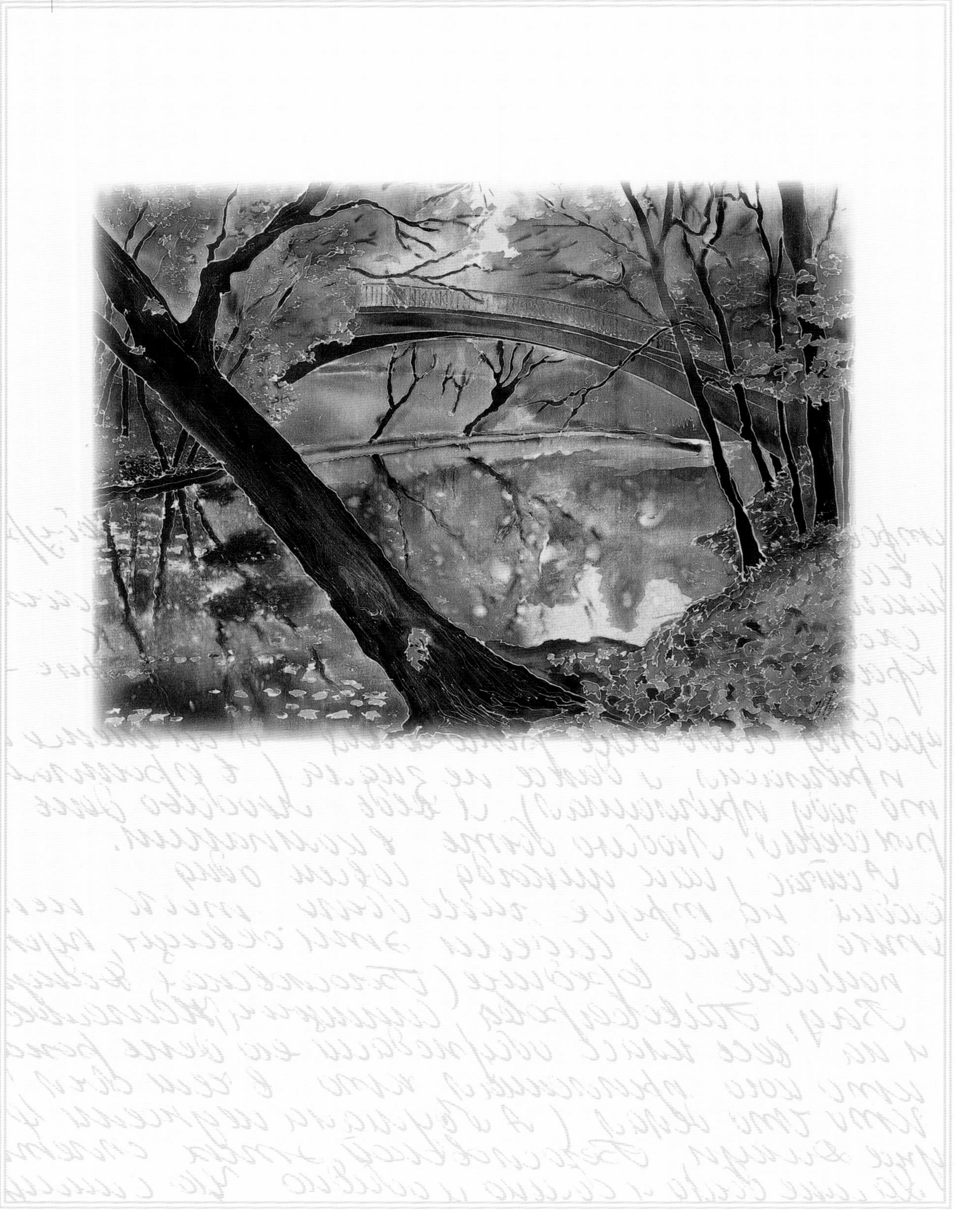

6 Obsession

When I came back from Pioneer camp, I felt a shift in the way Dima treated me. He had always teased me mercilessly, mocking me for writing in my diary like a schoolgirl. Suddenly, he would encourage me to write down the stories my grandmother had told me, and would even help me with them. Then, his mood shifting without warning to one of irritation, he corrected my efforts with a drawing pencil he had sharpened with a knife, creating deep furrows in the paper. He marred my tender heart, as well.

With the coming of autumn's wind and rain, his attitude became more and more belligerent. He began to pick arguments with me in public, calling me a "little fool." I wept silently.

Dima said that you were only living half a life unless you could handle strong emotions. He seemed to feed on conflict, and his great theme was that he was the only person who was awake to life. The rest of us were sleepwalking.

He would promise to meet me somewhere and not show up, just to keep me from becoming "complacent." I would trudge home through the wet leaves and rainy gutters that were our companions until winter arrived, vowing to stay away from his nasty moods until he apologized. But whenever he called me, my resolve weakened, and I would see him again. Of course, an apology from him was about as likely as snow in summertime.

One evening, there was a particularly rowdy party at his apartment, with vodka flowing as usual. Russian parties are always accompanied by plenty of drinking and singing, but this one was taking a dangerous turn. Some of Dima's army buddies were in town, and each one seemed determined to show the others that he could get drunker and sing louder than they could. Someone produced an old cardboard target and a gun. They nailed the target onto the wall and began taking pot shots at it, laughing uproariously when some of the other girls and I tried to get them to stop. I was furious. How could he treat me like this? I felt as if my love for him was getting smashed into the mud, like petals from a wilted bouquet tossed into the street. He didn't even pay any attention when I slipped away with a few friends. I resolved to stop seeing him, and felt very defeated.

Several days later Dima phoned, sorry that the party had gotten out of hand. His penitent attitude was such a shock to me that I wavered once more, and his suggestion that we take a trip together gave me reason enough to forgive him. Anyway, I wanted to go to the countryside before the heavy snows arrived. I told him about Suzdal and Kideksha and the wonderful camping trip Julia and I had taken with our school friends.

We decided to go the next weekend. Maybe if he saw Suzdal through my eyes, he would understand why I wanted to create beauty, rather than adopt his attitude that happiness was too commonplace an emotion.

After taking the bus from Vladimir, we got to Suzdal just as sunset reached its peak. Again, the exquisite pink light cast a warm glow on all the churches and towers of the holy district. Even Dima fell silent in the special atmosphere. Maybe things would get better between us after all.

We were getting hungry, so Dima offered to find us something to eat. All the restaurants had just closed, so he would have to beg for some bread at the back door of one of them. I wrapped myself tightly into my heavy coat and sat down on a bench outside a monastery wall to wait for him. Half an hour passed. Then an hour. It was really cold, since the sun had gone down, and I didn't know what to do. What had happened to him? Was he pulling another one of his stunts?

I decided to go back to the bus station, since at least I could stay warm there. I ran back and settled down on a wooden bench. Several more hours passed. I tried to sleep, but I was too angry. Finally, about two o'clock in the morning, I fell asleep for a few hours—then sat up to devour a hard-boiled egg I found in one of my pockets.

I felt a tugging on my sleeve. The sky was just a faint gray before dawn. Dima's green eyes danced in front of my face. Vodka and cigarette fumes choked me. "Hey, Natasha, I had a great time! This is a fantastic place. I ran into some incredible people and we had a little bit too much to drink. I tried to find you, but I got lost. Hey, what's the matter? So you had to sleep on a bench. Where's your sense of adventure?"

I choked on the egg as I tried to speak. Salty tears of frustration flowed freely from my eyes. He was oblivious, both to my suffering and to his part in it. He couldn't admit that he was just playing with me and indulging his nasty streak, and I realized that he had deserted me on purpose. The trip was ruined for me. I just wanted to get back on the bus and go home, but Dima knew how to twist my thoughts and confuse me.

Against my instincts, I relented. I knew I should walk away from his cruelty and mood swings, but I still loved this madman. His raw beauty and charisma still held me.

We stayed two days, camping out in a ruined monk's cell in one of the abandoned churches. Dima created wild, abstract paintings with a big palette knife and fortified himself with shots of cheap vodka. It began to rain—the kind of cold rain that chills you to your bones. This wasn't artistic and romantic. It was just depressing. I felt completely separate from him, knowing I could never depend on him for anything. We took the train back to Moscow in silence.

I didn't return his phone calls for weeks, and often soaked my pillow with tears; but I was determined to end this painful obsession. As I began to recognize the addictive quality of my love for him, I somehow understood that life with Dima was never going to get any better. The thought of marrying him never seriously crossed my mind. He was impossible.

I promised myself I would never live with this kind of love. It had come to seem like a terrible thing. Love could destroy people, and I didn't want to be destroyed. So I made a vow to myself. I would never let myself be captured by an obsessive love again. It was too dangerous—too uncontrollable. I would dedicate myself to my art. Art was safe. It would always be there for me. Art would never torture me, mock me, or die and leave me alone. Art would be my lover. From now on, the place in my heart that held the loved one would never be violated again.

I threw myself into my studies with a renewed energy. Everyone was amazed at the volume of work I began to produce. By that time, I had decided that I would concentrate on etching, and for the first time in my life, my stubbornness served me well. I never returned any of Dima's calls, and I avoided his neighborhood, even if it meant not going to my beloved Pushkin Museum for a while. Luckily, he seemed to have drifted away from the art school. I hoped I would never see him again.

Technique

The painting "Old Moscow Neighborhood" is one of my favorite cityscape pieces. It captures so much about my love of this old section of Moscow, with its elegant, crumbling facades, architectural richness, and quiet streets. By limiting my palette to very muted golds, rusty browns, and blues, I created a unity among the different shapes of the buildings that might be lacking if I rounded out the color choices more fully. It is always tempting to put too many colors in a painting, and a great deal can be learned from restricting the palette. It is a fine example of the old saying, "Less is more."

The large puddle of water is actually from a photograph I took somewhere else. I've added it to this painting to heighten the atmosphere of peacefulness, and made it into an inverted "v" to draw the viewer's eye back to building where Dima lived. The leaden grays of the sky and the cold gray street always remind me of the freeze I put on my love for Dima so that I could escape his hypnotic hold.

Old Moscow Neighborhood

7 Prague

Mid-winter in Moscow was like seeing the world on black and white television. Almost as soon as the snow fell, it turned various shades of dirty gray. The buildings were soot-stained, and the people shuffling between protective doorways were dressed in dark colors. Shoppers waited doggedly in queues, their heads wrapped in fur and wool, their faces muffled with scarves against the knife-sharp wind.

I stood at our apartment window, watching the gray world below. The phone rang, breaking the monotony of another dark evening. It was Nina, my mother's best friend. She had married a Czechoslovakian engineer and moved to Prague to live with him. Ninotchka invited me to visit them—to come and soak up some of Prague's great art and architecture. I was thrilled, as this would be my first chance to travel abroad.

Getting permission to travel outside of the borders of the Soviet Union followed an orderly, step-by-step process. Our first visit had to be to a socialist country such as Czechoslovakia to prove our political correctness. But when I went to apply for a visa, the reception I received was icy.

The balding, stooped man with an owl-like stare reminded me that my performance as Komsomol leader my first year at art school had been less than stellar. Komsomol leader? No one had wanted the job, and my classmates had taken advantage of my being away on a short painting trip to elect me to the post. I had never been interested in Party politics, limiting my activities in the youth organization to collecting the monthly dues. Suddenly I realized that this official was KGB, and he thought everything was political, especially a trip outside of the Soviet Union.

Mr. Owl also knew about the posters. Three students had gotten noisily drunk one night and turned a class assignment to make posters into a wild prank. They drew cartoons of Reagan and Brezhnev starting a military conflict because some idiot had installed the special red phones incorrectly. Laughing and stumbling over each other, they had nailed their posters up on several telephone poles and walls.

The next evening, they had been arrested. KGB officials had come to the school and had called me into the administrative offices to question and berate me. If I had been doing my job—identifying "amoral" influences among my school friends—I could have derailed this incident. All three students, including Alexei, one of my closest pals, had been expelled from the Art Institute, their future careers demolished.

Now this incident had come back to plague me. Mr. Owl rejected my application, and it ended up taking three years and countless appointments at the visa bureau before I was able to receive permission to travel to Czechoslovakia for just one summer.

Later on, the all-night train trip through Belorus and Poland to Europe would become a boring routine for me. But this first time, I found the endless delays at each border fascinating, and was too excited to sleep.

I began my explorations the next morning. Since both Nina and her engineer husband worked long hours at their jobs, I would be blissfully on my own. At every turn of her cobblestoned streets, Prague presented me with the magnificent architectural beauty of her old city center. Nestled between several hills, she lay glistening in the sun like a big, contented tabby cat—the broad Vltava River wrapped around her like a golden tail. One of the few Eastern European cities which had escaped being bombed into rubble in World War II, Prague is rich with beautifully restored Baroque, Gothic, and Art Nouveau buildings. Every fifteen steps or so, I had to sit down and sketch, while visitors from a dozen countries happily strolled the streets, laden with cameras and shopping bags. Music drifted out of cafes, restaurants, and pubs.

I emerged from a side street onto a wide pedestrian promenade by the river. A hulking bastion of stone, the Charles Bridge, arched before me—its span across the Vltava dramatically studded with huge, time-worn statues of saints. Throngs of tourists on the bridge mingled with musicians, puppeteers, artists with their paints and easels, performing dogs leaping through hoops.

Letting my intuition guide my steps, I was drawn as if by a magnet to the spiritual heart of Prague—Saint Vitus Cathedral—and stepped out of the bright sunlight into its cool, musty interior. After a few seconds, my eyes adjusted to the change. Moving slowly, as if in a trance, I gazed at forests of massive stone columns topped with a bower of intricately carved tracery, clusters of lifelike leaves and flowers that burst with the energy of spring blooms. I had seen pictures of Gothic cathedrals in the library at school, but that had not prepared me for the mystical experience of standing inside this holy space.

Tears of happiness welled up and blurred my vision as I arched my neck to view the stained glass windows. Of an almost unbelievable brilliance, these jewel-toned windows filtered the sunlight from outside, casting rainbows of misty, glowing color onto the grey stone of the cathedral's columns, arches, and royal tombs. Overwhelmed by so much pure beauty, and by my emotions, I had to leave after only a few minutes.

Suddenly I was starving. Around the corner from the cathedral, I stepped into a small corner store. Newspapers, magazines, and snacks were displayed in neat rows. What were these little cardboard cartons, decorated with lovely colored pictures of fruit? I chose one with lemons on it, gave the clerk a few coins, and went outside to sit on a bench and savor this new treat.

I rolled the first spoonful around my mouth. Milky smooth and sweet, the luscious dollop exploded with the taste of fresh lemons and awoke all my taste buds. So this was yogurt!

At home, dairy products were limited to the basics, such as milk and a few varieties of cheese. We had to go to a special dairy store for them, as we did for every food product in Moscow, and stand in line three times: once to place our order, once to pay for it, and finally to pick it up. The little carton of creamy lemon yogurt was the complete opposite of this frustrating process. Instantly available, sweet, cheap, and almost frivolously delicious, it stood for everything that was foreign and special and new. I jumped up eagerly after licking out the last drop, ready for more discoveries.

By the time I trudged back to Nina's home, I was in a rapture of artistic expression, with armloads of sketches and paintings in my satchel.

The next day, I wandered farther from the city center, and painted and sketched more churches and castles. Sitting by myself in a tree-filled park, I became aware of harmonica music being played from the far side of a grassy slope. I wandered in the direction of the music and found a tall, lanky fellow leaning against a tree. His worn jeans and road-battered hiking boots marked him as a fellow student and traveler.

Eric spoke no Russian, although he was from East Germany, and I no German, so we communicated in very limited English. I couldn't have found a better companion with whom to explore Prague. With his blue eyes, short white-blond hair, and unfailingly positive attitude, Eric was as uncomplicated as the sun.

Eric invited me to have a beer, but nothing in my life had prepared me for the experience of walking into a

Czech pub. Bars in Moscow were exclusive, dimly lit and relatively quiet. They were too expensive for my meager student stipend. Just the obligatory bribe at the entrance was a month worth of lunches and supplies. Here, however, scores of long wooden tables were filled with locals and tourists, happily downing gigantic, foaming glasses of beer. Dozens of different beers! Tall bottles of light and dark lagers—from glistening, golden ambers to rich, deep, smoky browns—left sticky rings on all the polished wooden surfaces.

Tables full of German students were singing loudly, yelling, laughing at jokes—being foolish in public. At home, our entire social life was carried on in private, usually around the kitchen table, or at the dacha in the countryside. There would be singing and stories and jokes, but never in a public place. We would have been arrested.

After a quick pub-crawl, limited by our purses, I invited Eric to go look at the stained glass windows of Saint Vitus Cathedral. It was late in the afternoon, and gray, puffy clouds were scudding across the sky, promising rain. This time, the light from the windows pouring onto the stone carvings of the columns had a completely different quality—muted and subtle. The revelation of this difference would bring me back again and again to paint, like Monet, at different times of the day.

In the newer part of the cathedral, six tall stained glass windows hung in perfection around a glorious rose window, each in a different style. Alfons Mucha, the father of the Czech Art Nouveau style, had designed one of them, hand-painting each piece of glass to achieve the subtle colorations for which he was famous. Two years later, I created my first piece of wearable hand-painted clothing using these windows as my inspiration.

Sometimes I would spend my days alone—at other times, in the company of Eric. We developed a light, effortless relationship, tinged with romantic feeling. It was such a treat to be friends with this easygoing fellow, so different from Dima, with his moods and tirades. Eric and I would find a comfortable tree in a park to sit under, and he would play his harmonica while I painted or sketched.

To our mutual surprise, the parks and streets of Prague were lined with fruit trees. In the bright summer sun, lusciously ripe pears and apples dangled within arm's reach, waiting to be plucked and devoured. The long golden afternoons spent lying under apple trees, painting the magnificent panoramas of buildings, made me feel as if I were Eve, in the original Paradise.

At that time in my life, Prague's effect on me was almost totally visual. It was where I began my lifelong love affair with painting cityscapes and the details of buildings. I knew little about the battle-darkened centuries of history that the lovely, seductive city had witnessed. And it wasn't until much later, in Brussels, when I saw the film *The Unbearable Lightness of Being,* that I learned—to my shock and shame—that Russian tanks had mowed down civilians in the streets of Prague in 1968.

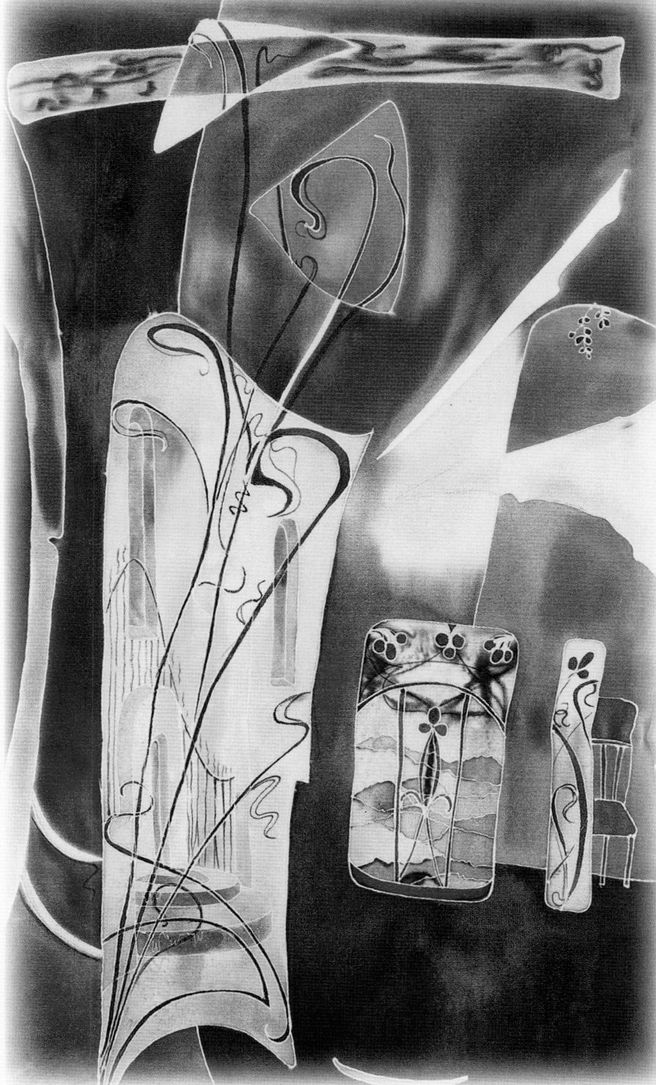

In Moscow, we had heard only the vaguest of rumors.

By the end of my six-week stay, I felt as if I were a local. Visitors asked me for directions, and I pulled out my maps and sent them on their way. When some German tourists bought one of my sketches for the equivalent of fifteen dollars, I was dizzy with success: maybe I would be able to make my living as an artist!

Buying art supplies in Prague was a Russian artist's dream. In Moscow, if I was lucky, someone who was a member of the Artist's Union would sneak me into the Art League store. I would very quietly point at something I wanted, and they would buy it for me. Here, there were rows and rows of paints, smooth wooden boxes of high-quality pastel colors, sleek sable brushes. Even the erasers smelled better in Prague. I brought home as many treasures as I could afford.

Everyone expected me to spend every ruble on shopping before I returned home. So the day before I was to leave, I spent the last of my money on a pinkish-orange fur coat of dyed squirrel. My odd choice certainly disappointed my more practical mother, but I made the heads of gray-clad Muscovites turn for years afterward. In the hideous fur, I looked like a huge candle flame, or a lioness on LSD.

The drawings and paintings I did in Prague were the basis for my final portfolio for graduation: a presentation of forty etchings of my favorite buildings and churches. Prague was a great source of inspiration for me, and I felt as if I were the first one to experience her magical quality. Now, of course, thousands of travelers have discovered my secret treasure of a city.

Technique

As a student, I was really in love with etching, expressing myself best with fine hatchings of black lines. Once I began painting on silk, I created "Study in Gray." You might expect that my paintings of Prague would reflect the golden apples, boisterous pubs, and illuminated stained glass windows of my summer visit. But strange as it may seem, I have never been inspired by brightly colored days, and have not painted them until very recently. I preferred the moodiness and depth of overcast days, with their opportunities to paint reflections, and the myriad colors of snow have inspired me to paint many winter scenes. These tones allowed me to paint my emotions and my sense of the underlying spirituality of cities far more successfully than if I used pure, brilliant colors.

In "Study in Gray" I chose to paint the Charles Bridge and its watchtower after a light snow. There are shades of every color in this painting—pinks and blues and greens and yellows—but I have mixed them, toned them down, and grayed them to create a muted palette. Back in Moscow years later, painting only on silk, I would always be most drawn to painting the frozen world of winter snows and the blue-lavender shadows of rain-splashed scenes.

Study in Gray

8 Riga

The weathered stone buildings of Riga's old town center were huddled over the narrowest of cobblestoned streets like the irregular, blackened teeth of an ancient crone's grin. In this Hans Christian Andersen storybook setting, I discovered the richly creative life of a flourishing artists' community.

My mother was to attend a chemical research conference in Latvia's capital and had asked me if I would like to accompany her on the three day trip. Of course I would! I had awakened early in the tiny but comfortable hotel room while my mother still slept. We had arrived at night, so I had no idea what it was like outside the heavy hotel drapes that blanketed our window and protected us from the mid-winter chill. I pulled aside the dark green velvet and saw magic embodied in ice and stone.

Our modern hotel had been built on the western side of the Daugava River. Across the silver ribbon of river, whose banks were carpeted with fresh white snow, the slate-roofed buildings of Old Riga were silhouetted in black against a brilliant, pink-orange dawn sky. The color graduated upward from the horizon with an unearthly clarity—from yellow to bright pink to an intense cerulean blue.

I quietly got out my brushes and watercolors and began to paint what I saw, spreading out my stiff water color paper on the floor next to my sleeping mother. Frustrated, I realized that the vivid colors of the sky at sunrise or sunset always looked garish on paper, no matter how beautiful they

really were. This was my first experience of what would later become my manifesto: to look for beauty in unexpected places, not in postcard-perfect scenery.

For three days and evenings, while my mother attended the conference, I was on my own, trudging through the snowy streets in a trance of inspiration and wonder. For centuries, Riga had been a medieval German trade center, through which flowed all the riches of Russia—her furs, hides, honey, and amber. Whole rows and blocks of winding streets were virtually untouched since the seventeenth century and gave the old center of the city its fairy-tale quality.

But it was the life of this magical place that struck me even more than the extraordinarily beautiful buildings. There was music coming out of bars and cafes, there was talking and gay laughter, and couples were kissing in doorways. Through frost-etched windows, I could see artists working in their studios, surrounded by paintings, ceramics, and carvings. I wanted more than anything to be one of them.

I did piles and piles of pen-and-ink sketches on that first trip to Latvia. Returning to Moscow, I did a very large pen-and-ink drawing, which I still have today. While in Riga, I had the odd sensation of floating over the city—not being a part of its life. So I did my drawing as if I were viewing the Dome Cathedral in the old city's center from up high, with four streets radiating out from it. I filled the sky, Van Gogh style, with lots of little black spirals. Each stroke of the pen—each detail that I drew—made me feel as if I were back on those snowy streets again. It's as if had fallen in love with Riga and was pining away for my new, distant lover.

There is no way to tell the story of my adventures in Riga without introducing my Moscow friend, Armo. And it is impossible for me to think about Armo without giggling appreciatively at his cartoon-like character.

Armo Avetisian was a huggable Armenian mountain bear of a man. His full beard and wild, black Einstein hair were made even more amusing by his Armenian-accented Russian. Everything about Armo was bigger than life, except his stubby bear legs. He collected women's phone numbers in his dog-eared black address book like notches on a hunter's bow, and charmed and dazzled me, making me laugh non-stop at his comical appearance and grand-opera personality.

Armo had set himself up in an outrageous artist's studio and love-nest right next to Red Square. I'm surprised he never got arrested just for being too flamboyant, not to mention the illegal fireplace he had somehow managed to vent through an unused duct.

When I went to one of Armo's very noisy, very big parties, the first thing that struck me was a blast of heat from the fireplace. The light from the flames would dance off walls he had painted a brilliant Chinese red, and I would start sweating the second I walked in and tossed my coat onto the towering pile of outerwear on the bed. Every inch of the high-ceilinged studio was covered with Armo's huge, flamboyant paintings: brilliantly-colored abstracts and great fleshy nudes in come-hither poses. Armo's erotic imagination was displayed on his studio walls.

Armo's wild parties in his Moscow digs had been more than just excuses to drink and sing. The only way to survive the bleakness and bureaucratic control stifling our daily lives was to have lots of friends. They could help you make connections, find deals and opportunities, and would share with each other whatever clout they had in the system. And for Armo, of course, friends were a way to increase the flow of women through his doorway and his chances of making a conquest. Or so he thought.

For one of his birthday parties, he had invited about fifty women and two men. It was November, and a great whirling blizzard was filling the streets outside with drifts of new, crystalline snow. Everyone was having a great time. Someone had brought conga drums and the guests danced and laughed for hours. As the fun reached a feverish peak, Armo had to go out for more firewood, but everyone took his departure as a cue to leave.

I decided to stay a little longer, and when Armo returned, he and I started sharing stories about

our travel adventures. I told him how Riga had entranced me, with its flourishing artists' community and medieval stone buildings.

Armo said he knew someone in Riga I could stay with, and pulled out his black address book with a grand gesture, like some rock impresario with great connections. He found a woman's number, and in an instant we were on the phone.

I had met Marita before in Moscow, but didn't know her well enough to just show up on her doorstep. But Armo's dynamic personality was unstoppable, and I was able to return to Riga with a place to stay.

Marita's brother and a friend of his met me at the railroad station and told me that Marita was in the hospital for some minor surgery. Since she would be at her aunt's house for several weeks to recover, I could stay in her studio for as long as I wanted.

The boys walked me through the narrow streets of Old Riga, familiar to me from my first trip with my mother. They helped me carry my bags up the steep, worn, wooden staircase to Marita's apartment in the slant-walled attic of the old Mansard building that faced the Dome Cathedral square. Then they left me by myself to settle in.

I walked over to the window. How is it that I recognized this view? I had been in this room before a hundred times in my dream life. Though I had always been blessed with many beautiful dreams, none was more beautiful to me than this recurring one—the fairy tale to outshine all fairy tales. I was back again! There was the green glass bottle on the windowsill and the starry night framed by the chimneys and rooftops. There was a woman reflected in the mirror with a thick black frame. And here were the same collections of dried flowers and shells, an old rocking chair, paintings everywhere. The silence was broken by only two sounds: the ticking of the antique French clock on the wall—its sweet music chiming out the hour—and the squeaking of the weather vane on the dome of the cathedral close by.

For the next three weeks, I painted in my absent friend's studio. In the afternoons and evenings, Marita's brother took me around to visit the other artists. He knew everyone: the potters, painters, glass blowers, and sculptors. Now it was possible to be part of the expansive artists' life in Old Riga I had yearned for on that first visit with my mother. Every day there were great conversations about art and life, a bottle of wine, and the forging of warm friendships and life-long connections. This was the life I had read about in books, like the artists of Montmartre in Paris. People would drop in without any invitation, then go off together to see another artist and view their latest work. My imagination and creativity were stimulated constantly—it was like being on some kind of art inspiration drug. I returned to Moscow overflowing with possibilities and ideas.

The next spring, I got a call from Armo. He told me that there was a fabulous art festival every year in Riga called *Makslas Dienas*, or "Days of Art." The whole town would be partying and celebrating.

At that time, I had a studio in the Petrovka section of Moscow and I had developed a set of art groupies, a whole flock of guys hanging out with their "artist friend Natasha." They heard about my plans for Makslas Dienas and decided to come along. I also invited two of my French girlfriends,

Marie-Claire and Monique, even though their visas didn't allow them to travel legally. We shamelessly charmed the guards at the border crossings and managed not to land in detention.

The event had been advertised for weeks with beautifully designed posters that hung all over the town. The whole center of Old Riga was turned over to the artists, and they could display their art anywhere—on the walls of public buildings, on easels, and in the middle of the square.

All the artists outdid themselves with their most colorful, creative work. Marita did a portrait of me wearing a brilliant fuchsia-pink sweater and turquoise pants. She decorated it all over with glittery gold paint, and glued six-inch-long earrings right onto the painting—one fuchsia, the other turquoise. Then she displayed it on the front of the Dome Cathedral. Another ceramicist friend created a giant cake with pink frosting and seven tiers, called "The Joy of Life": an arm protruded from its middle holding a giant sausage. And store mannequins were painted green and blue and grouped together in front of the cathedral with ceramic fruits and flowers sprouting from their shoulders like wings.

For the whole week, life was a round of parties, music, great art, and plenty of drinking—a bacchanalian celebration of spring, creativity, and excess. One artists' association had rented a whole restaurant, and converted it into "A Night at the Italian Opera." Mozart's *Magic Flute* poured from the sound system, a lavish spread of food was laid out, and everyone came dressed in farcically comic and overdone costumes, with purple velvet and taffeta-draped drag queens swishing through the crowds to rounds of laughter and applause.

Later, I would show slides of these celebrations, as well as hundreds of slides of buildings and churches, to my friends in Moscow, accompanied by plenty of vodka and some precious cans of shrimp, my favorite food treat. We dubbed these evenings "Slides and Shrimp"; but I would enthusiastically show so many details of Riga's ancient buildings to my patient friends that their eyes would begin to close, and I realized that the shrimp was the bigger draw.

For several years, I came back to Riga each spring for "Days of Art." Usually, Armo would be there, and more and more of my friends from Moscow came with us. These were the happiest, most carefree days of my student life. And if I needed a new place to stay and my address book couldn't provide it, there was always Armo's book.

Riga became a second home for me. I always thought that if for some reason I could no longer live in Moscow, I would move to Riga and live there the rest of my days.

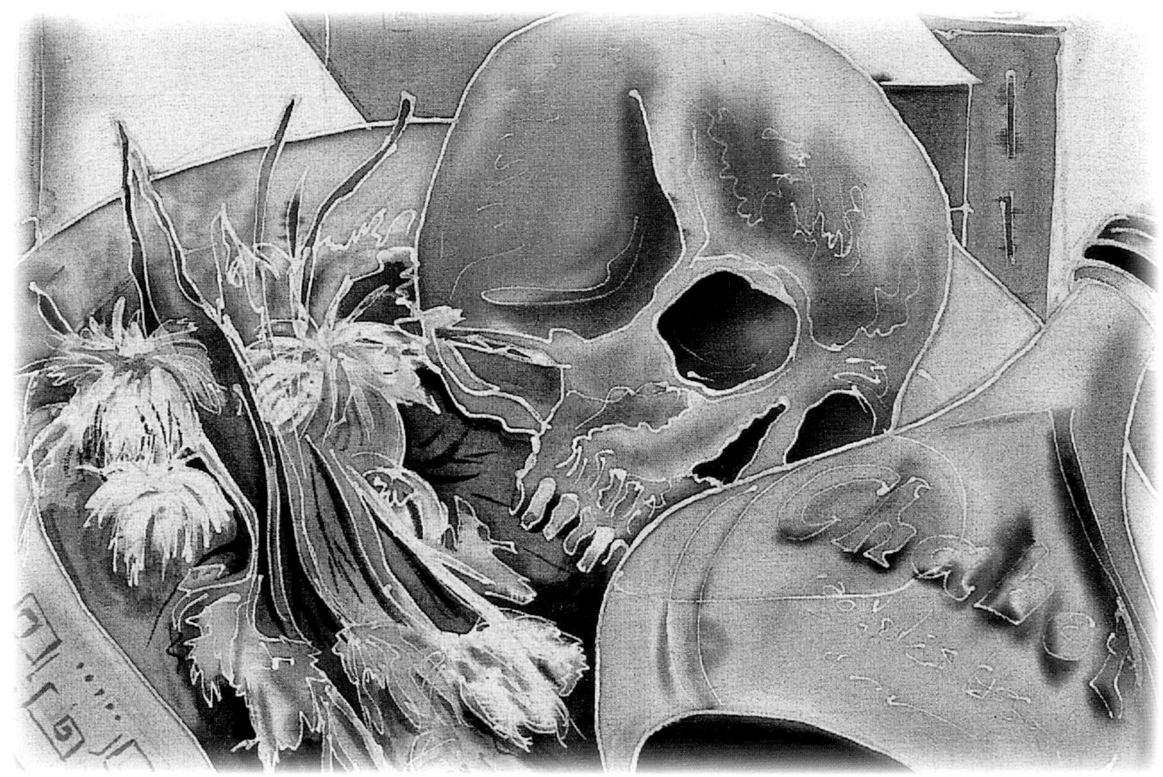

Technique

This painting from my Riga days called "Snowy Rooftops, Riga" was inspired by a still life Marita had set up on the windowsill in her studio. I added a winter view of the rooftops from another photograph I had in my files. What's most difficult about painting winter is successfully capturing all the subtle shades of white in the snow. I had learned from one of my teachers to hold a piece of white paper up against a landscape element that appears white so I could see that pure white does not exist in nature. The "white" areas will always reflect color from the things around them.

The wet on wet technique, which I used to paint in the shadows on the top of the skull, is the most difficult process to control. (The skull in this painting does have some structural lines indicated by the gutta resist.) To work on a white area, I wet the entire area to be shaded and then wait until the surface has exactly the right degree of dampness before adding the shadowing colors. I patiently test the wet area with the edge of my palm until I feel just a damp coolness. Then I have no more than ten minutes, depending on the temperature of my studio, to seize the moment and add my shadows. Taking a very dry brush, I rub in—rather than paint—the pale shadows, adding tiny bits of dye so that the whole area does not get flooded with color. There should be just enough moisture to allow the edges of the shadows to be soft.

Snowy Rooftops, Riga

9 Darkness & Light

The first few years after I graduated from the Art Institute, I was wildly excited about everything artistic, and experimented eagerly in several different media. One week I was splashing through reams of water color paper; the next, I was smeared with oil paint. To be a serious artist, however, I knew I needed to settle down and concentrate, so I began working exclusively in etching and ceramics—my favorites from college days.

Both art forms involved working with very toxic materials like zinc and lead. But no one was worrying about health hazards in those days—from the Party down to the factory workers—and warning labels were nonexistent. Furthermore, no materials were available in art stores except for people who were members of the elite Artists' Union. So I would haunt the back doors of ceramics factories, make friends with sympathetic workers, and then barter for bits of leftover glazes.

Since our studio spaces were not equipped with appropriate ventilation, I got terrible headaches from my constant exposure to fumes. And one rainy November evening, my mother got a phone call from the hospital: "Ada Mihailovna, your daughter is dead."

Fortunately, my mother refused to accept this dreadful message. She knew the Soviet bureaucracy too well to believe anything until she had checked it out with her own sources.

I had been taken to the emergency room after collapsing on the floor of my studio. Drifting in and out of consciousness, I heard bits and pieces of information: "complete dysfunction of the liver, acute infectious hepatitis . . . she'll never come out of it . . ." On the bed not a half meter away from me lay a young man—completely naked—who had overdosed on drugs, and he quietly died a few hours later. It really broke my spirit when I overheard the student nurses saying that I would be next.

As it turned out, I had contracted the hepatitis when my blood had been drawn in preparation for the job as the ceramics teacher at Pioneer camp; the clinic, like many others in Russia, was always short on supplies and had been reusing its needles. The exposure to toxic chemicals had further weakened my liver, so that it was severely compromised.

My mother went into action. As a chemical engineer, she had old school friends who worked in the laboratories of various hospitals. Her friend Elizaveta explained that the doctors had told her I was dead because they didn't want to admit they couldn't save me.

With desperate persistence, my mother repeatedly called the hospital until she got through to one of the attending doctors—a Doctor Sholokov—and begged him to tell her if anything at all could be done. Well, there was one drug that might possibly save her only daughter, he said. It was an American drug called interferon. But he didn't have any, nor could he obtain it, and it was extraordinarily expensive. "But then again, Ada Mihailovna, if you know someone at Department 4. . ."

My mother knew exactly what he meant. Department 4 was the Kremlin's hospital, but everyone had referred to it in this oblique manner since Stalin's time, when it was imperative to pretend to know as little about the government as possible. Department 4 had all the best doctors, imported medicines, and the latest technology—all reserved for Party officials. No one was supposed to know that the Communist Party provided a whole subculture of special schools, medical and vacation facilities, restaurants, stores, and supermarkets for the Party elite. But of course everyone knew.

Sholokov told my mother I would need ten shots of interferon to boost my immune system to the point that my liver might recover. Each shot would cost her half a month's salary—if she could find someone to sell it to her under the table.

After calling everyone she knew, my mother finally got the phone number of a friend's friend who worked in the Kremlin hospital, and purchased the interferon. Now, living near me in San Francisco, she still won't tell me exactly how she managed it.

But what about our famous free medical care? Yes, on a day-to-day basis, we got much better treatment than what passes for health care through my current HMO. Family doctors made house calls for common colds and flu, and were very good at hands-on treatment. The hospitals, however, were a different story. We Russians used to joke with friends at the kitchen table, "Free medicine? Sure, they'll kill you for free. . ." With constant scarcities of high-tech machines and medicines, patients and their families had to make survival their personal project.

My mother slipped past the wooden-faced attendant at the front desk and brought the interferon to me in the intensive care unit of the contagious ward, which was strictly off-limits to visitors. It was staffed by young nurses who, in return for free schooling, were required to work at tough, low-paying medical jobs for three years. They hated their jobs and had only two goals: to survive the grave dangers of the ward and to find a husband with a good job who could lift them out of their near-poverty. Disease could bring anyone to the contagious ward, and the hospital turned a blind eye to the frequent romantic liaisons between nurses and their patients.

Even in my semiconscious stupor, I was convinced that I needed to be vigilant or I would die. Once I noticed an air bubble in my IV tube, and managed to get someone to fix it. But it frightened me badly, and I would stay awake all night watching for another bubble, while the nurses and their potential mates coupled furtively in deserted labs. Only one older nurse could change the position of the needle without leaving my so arm full of holes that it looked like some satanically-possessed woodpecker had attacked me.

My mother was my guardian and defender, incessantly badgering the hospital staff to make things better for me. Since the administration there knew very well that she could have made a loud protest about the fact that they had told her I was dead when I wasn't, they let her bribe her way into the forbidden contagious ward whenever she could manage it.

First, she had me moved out of a freezing-cold room populated by two ninety-year old ladies dying of something that made them cough and hack incessantly, while an indescribably gross, greenish-black ooze dripped from the ceiling onto my bed. We took to calling the first room "the seventh circle of Hell."

However, the depressing horror show was not without its moments of comic relief. Because my liver was under such stress, I wasn't supposed to eat anything for the first two weeks. But my mother felt so badly for me that she decided to smuggle in some of my favorite food, and tiptoed dramatically into my room one day armed with a small electrical appliance for boiling water, and a single raw shrimp. Then, guarding the door to make sure no one was coming, she set up the clandestine device on a small table and covered it with her overcoat.

Unfortunately, Dr. Lubov was making his rounds and walked in exactly as she was serving my weeny little shrimp on a napkin. She might as well have been a madwoman administering a dose of poison: he tore the forbidden feast from her hands, and I laughed and then cried until the tears soaked my pillow.

A week later, my family tried to smuggle me out of the hospital so I could spend New Year's Eve with them as it was our favorite holiday. I was very depressed and the lack of sleep was making me almost insane, so my mother thought it would cheer me up to have a day at home and a chance to phone my friends.

Early that holiday evening, when many of the hospital staff were already slugging vodka, my parents "borrowed" a gurney and secretly sneaked onto my ward. But the ever-vigilant Dr. Lubov again ruined my mother's plans. Bursting suddenly out of the staff room like a jack-in-the box, he threatened them wildly with punishments that were probably beyond his capacity to carry out.

Then my friend Gennady, who was seeing my best girlfriend Anna, began to brighten my days in the hospital. He was an unforgettable character, like Armo, the Armenian bear, but his complete opposite. A very short, muscular fellow, he was strikingly handsome. And because of his diminutive size, he had all his clothes custom-made, including a perfectly crafted, pint-sized leather briefcase. He was a successful black marketeer and an excellent trickster who could talk his way past the gates of heaven.

Genna showed up in the lobby of the hospital dressed in a perfectly-tailored set of doctor's whites and sternly introduced himself as Gennady Joffe, Director of the Infectious Diseases Department at Virashky Central Hospital. He ordered the attendant to take him immediately to the contagious ward.

Maybe it was the luxurious leather brief case that stunned the attendants. In any case, Genna was ushered right up to my room, where he gave orders to change my bedding and bring me special tropical fruit juices. And a few weeks later, as if risking a major upset in his comfortable life hadn't been enough, he coached my girlfriend Anna on how to behave like a nurse, got her a set of nurse's whites, and slipped her past the sleepy stare of the front-desk attendant for another clandestine visit to my room.

When I was finally released from the hospital, it was the middle of winter, and I was deeply depressed. I couldn't eat anything but the mildest of foods, and drinking alcohol was totally forbidden. Again, Genna came to the rescue: if he saw me reaching for a wine glass, he would grab it and drink the wine himself.

He and his friend Losha were two brotherly angels and constant companions during my recovery. Genna's black market dealings out of his engineering office gave him ample monetary resources, and he loved to share his largesse with friends. On my first day home, he and Losha took me to Moscow's most expensive seafood restaurant to cheer me up, even though I couldn't eat much, and Losha despised fish. The waiter's face wore an expression of utter disbelief when he realized that two of his three customers would be eating nothing. There were at least fifty people passing by on the sidewalk outside who would never have the remotest chance of eating in such posh surroundings.

Then, after a giddy impromptu visit to the horse races, where we lost a considerable chunk of Genna's black market earnings for the week, my pals returned me to my frantic mother six hours late. Genna had told her we were going out for "a little walk and some fresh air."

For a long time afterward, when people would ask me about my illness, I would burst into tears. It took ten years for the physical and mental scars to heal. Never again would I feel so helplessly out of control. Only the love of friends and family had kept me going during those years of recovery.

I was now desperate to find some way I could practice my art, without again working with toxic materials, which would have been akin to signing my own death warrant. Art was the central passion of my existence.

Then I remembered a short course in silk painting I had taken at the Art Institute. In Russia, as it is to some degree here in the States, silk painting is considered a decorative art, an inferior cousin of the fine arts. But I knew that silk dyes were not as toxic as the materials used for etching and ceramics, so I began to spend my long recuperation painting on silk.

Driven to make the medium perform for me, I took all my experience as a fully-formed artist and transformed it onto silk. Doggedly pulling out old etchings and pastels, I reworked them as silk paintings, and felt my creativity catch on fire. I was endlessly amazed at the beauty of the dyes as they flowed over the pure white silk, staining the fabric like a river slowly flooding its banks. The serene, meditative quality of the process was healing, and it restored my sense of myself as an artist.

Since then, I have exclusively painted on silk, and have ignored pressure from the art gallery world to use my talents for something more traditional and acceptable, like oils or water color. Perhaps my singleminded loyalty to the medium comes from my associating painting on silk with recovering from the illness which almost ended my life.

During this period of renewed creativity, I did several self-portraits on silk, including "Self-Portrait With Skull." I had always loved skulls, so when my mother found one at her lab, dusty and unused, I begged her to let me have it. Transfixed by its beauty—the subtle play of smooth and sharp edges, and the golden glow of the polished bone—I kept the skull on my bedside table. I would light a ring of candles around it, and watch it in the flickering shadows. By then, my family was accustomed to my eccentricities, and knew I wasn't experimenting with black magic. The skull simply served me as a window into the mystery of life and death.

Having come close to death, I was no longer frightened by it. In fact, the near-death experience, instead of scaring me, convinced me that I was meant to live boldly and fearlessly. There could be no other reason I was still walking around and breathing.

We Russians have a fatalistic attitude towards death: "When your number is up, it's up, so don't worry about it." But no painting of mine with a skull in it—no matter how technically masterful—has ever sold. Perhaps I am always more willing than others to be reminded of death's constant presence.

Technique

Because one little brushful of too-wet dye can transform a goddess into Quasimodo, the painting of faces puts the technique of painting during "the perfect dampness window of opportunity," (described in the previous technique section), to its ultimate test.

You should practice sketching faces from life with pencil and paper, until you increase your skills at it; even better, sketch facial muscles and bones from an anatomical text. These two exercises will give you the confidence you need for sketching the features of the face in soft pencil (4B to 6B) on silk before you begin painting.

Your goal is to paint the whole face without a single resist line, because the resist would give it a harsh, cartoon-like quality.

For "Self Portrait With Skull" I first mixed the flesh color of the face, using water, magenta, yellow, and a little bit of dried up purple or black from a palette from my last week's painting session. (You should learn to keep a box full of little bottles of dried-up dyes handy for a number of silk painting techniques.) I applied the flesh color to the face.

Again, I waited until the face section was cool to the touch of the back of my hand, but not wet. Using a stiff, small synthetic bristled brush (#1 or #2), I added the shadows which contour the cheeks, eyes, forehead, and nose, painting a little bit less than the area to be shaded, as the dye still spread a little. Then, with a brush that was barely wet, I used dried-up dyes exclusively. I reserved the deepest shadows for the area above the eyes, using my knowledge that the human eye is a round object in a deep socket. I kept defining the key outlines of the eyes and mouth until I was almost working dry. Finally, I touched up my work with an old, half dried-up gray or black fine tipped marker.

I always recommend to my students that they paint the face in a painting first, so that if it is ruined, they haven't lost all the rest of their work. I guess I like to live dangerously. I always paint the face last.

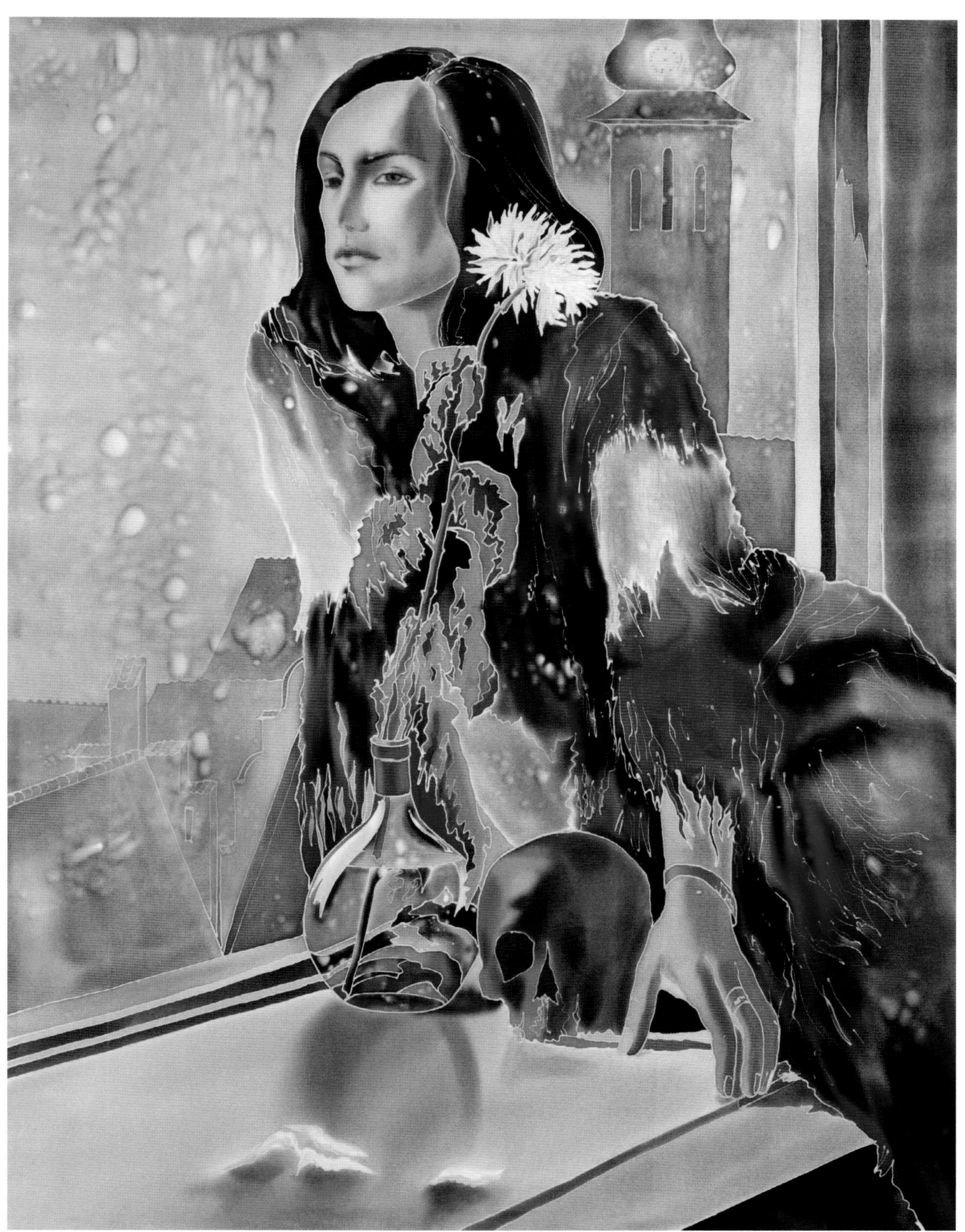

Self Portrait with Skull

10 Mon Amour Natasha

When a pudgy, slightly balding French tourist introduced himself to me in the Ancient Greek Sculpture hall of the Pushkin Art Museum, I know now that I should have run screaming for the nearest exit.

It was several years before my life-threatening illness. I had never met anyone who came from farther away than Poland, and talking to any foreigner was a forbidden and exciting adventure for a first-year art student. With his neatly pressed blue jeans and a leather jacket stretched tightly over his fat little belly, he seemed at least to be a man of means, if a slightly dull-looking one.

At any rate, in those days we were all crazy for anything unattainably French—and had been ever since Peter the Great donned ruffled shirts and became Russia's first completely obsessed Francophile. Our gloomy Muscovite humor made us smirk ironically when a busy friend joked that she couldn't meet for lunch because she had to "fly to Paris on urgent business. . ."

Through a few tentative words of shared English, and a lot of pantomime, I learned that twenty-six-year-old Etienne was in the newspaper business, lived in fabled seaside Biarritz, and was on an art tour of Moscow and St. Petersburg. We chatted for a few hours, exchanged addresses (as chance acquaintances sometimes do) and promised to write (which no one ever does).

But Etienne wrote. And wrote. In fact, he wrote me—through the painstaking translations of a Russian-born co-worker—once a month for the next three years, though he did not receive a single reply. Determined as only a man hopelessly in love can be, he prayed that his letters would elude the censors, and that I would respond.

When the Soviet system started coming unglued, about three years after we had first met, a few of Etienne's letters began to slip through. And after *perestroika* started making steady progress, more letters arrived each year, and I responded to them. Finally, he asked if he could visit me. Why not? I thought. After graduating from the Art Institute, I was bored with my first compulsory job, teaching in a bleak and suffocatingly dull primary school. The children were indifferent to art and I felt like I was in jail, serving my sentence. Life needed a little spicing up.

Etienne's first visits took place on park benches, in museums, or standing in Red Square. I would bring along a few friends who were studying French and wanted to meet "a real French person." He expressed his fanatic devotion to me by signing up each summer for Russian art tours, although I realized he didn't give a fig about art and knew nothing about it. But I rather enjoyed the idea of his pursuit: it was flattering and intriguing. Inevitably, the KGB started harassing me for "consorting with a foreigner" and told the school's director that I was a bad apple, a rotten influence on the pure morals of our sweet Soviet youth. I was excited about the prospect of being fired, because I was creating art and teaching private students in my own studio by then, and this would give me the opportunity to be a full-time artist.

But I didn't get fired. The KGB just kept calling me, now insisting that I marry Etienne: they had realized that they could turn my risky behavior into a nice opportunity for themselves. I started feeling the chill of their attentions, and thanks to my French friend, my prospects for a career in the Soviet Union were beginning to look bleak. I also knew that I would probably never be allowed to go abroad on my own.

I liked Etienne well enough, but even after several visits, I hardly knew him. He was painfully unsociable with my friends—a classic nerd. And I had obviously become his obsession. By then he had pursued me for an astounding seven years, hinting frequently about marriage.

Would this stodgy fellow be my passport to the West? I had just undergone a spectacular breakup with a serious boyfriend, and was feeling desperate. So the prospect of seeing France pulled at me like a glittering, bejeweled magnet. I figured that I could always return to Moscow if our connection didn't work out.

Finally, one bitterly cold and rainy day, as we huddled under his umbrella, I agreed to the latest in Etienne's string of marriage proposals. And after endless bureaucratic hassles, a marriage day was set. There would be a simple ceremony in the registry office.

When my mother and I drove out to the airport to meet my future husband's flight, we were completely surprised by the wedding outfit in the huge box Etienne carried, as well as the arrival of Etienne's bustling little mother.

Madame Cotard's manic energy was draining. Oblivious to our surroundings, she opened the bursting box to display its precious contents. Of course the dress was "perfect, perfect, perfect!" Didn't I adore the three layers of poufy netting, the bouquet of artificial orange blossoms, the garter (I had never seen one before), the gloves, the white satin shoes, the hat, and the veil?

I protested: there was no way I was going to wear this nightmare of a wedding-day fantasy! But the adrenaline-fueled trilling of Madame prevailed. Etienne had spent several months' salary on the silly outfit, and they won.

Then, because I would never fit into my father's tiny, battered Moskovich wearing this mound of whipped fluff, we had to scramble to find a friend who could borrow a sleek black Chaika sedan and a driver who could leave his government office for a few hours. This under-the-table arrangement cost several hundred well-placed rubles.

The circus had come to town, but unfortunately *we* were the clowns, trapeze artists, and

trained seals. Etienne had forgotten to bring his passport, and we drove the Chaika in crazed circles around Red Square, looking for his tour guide, Tanya, because she was holding everyone's documents. For what reason, I scoffed? To keep meek little tourists from escaping into the arms of mother Russia?

The chauffeur felt so sorry for me that he broke open the insanely expensive bottle of French cognac we had bought for him as a tip, and started nursing me with slugs of the precious liquid to calm my frazzled nerves. If we were late, we would blow the whole plan, because Etienne's tour had to leave for St. Petersburg the next day with me in tow. The plan, arranged somehow by the French tour leader, was that I would pretend to be part of the tour group, since as a Russian citizen, I was forbidden to enter any of the fancy hotels catering to foreigners.

Two hours later, we found Tanya and Etienne's passport, and arrived at the doors of the registry office. Someone had distributed more rubles in the right places, and the registrar had re-scheduled our appointment.

Little Genna was at the curb to help me get out of the car. We kept passing him armloads of tulle until he was completely buried, and I began to giggle drunkenly at the sight of him swallowed up by a dress.

By then, the guests had become so nervous about our non-appearance that they had drunk all their celebratory vodka and were completely smashed. I myself don't recall a thing about the actual ceremony. I was numb.

The circus atmosphere continued at St. Petersburg's most expensive hotel, where swarms of Russian black marketeers and fur-draped prostitutes crowded the hallways, trying to buy jeans, exchange currency, or offer their services. Mr. Levi Strauss would have been pleased that European and American jeans topped the list of Western goods Russians craved the most, and a lively underground trade in jeans was flourishing. A hefty cut of the profits from these transactions had silenced the

normally vigilant doormen. But I struggled to suppress my laughter when they tried to wheel and deal with me, thinking I was French.

The French tourists were offended when they were given only mineral water at dinner. What about "*vin rouge avec du viande?* Are these people barbarians?" I was kept busy making forays out to the Beryozka stores for foreigners, using my classroom French to pick out mediocre Georgian wines for the horrified gourmets. Then the French, thumbs over half-finished wine bottles, joined the prostitutes in the hallways and partied from room to room.

The second evening, Etienne's tour group wanted to celebrate our wedding Russian-style by drinking vodka with us. But I couldn't figure out why they were pouring orange juice into the glasses, and had only one bottle of vodka for twelve people—I had never seen a mixed drink in my life.

Laughing nervously, I explained that when Russians drank, there were usually three or four people to several bottles of vodka, and no oranges, since the nearest ones were in an orchard on the Black Sea, several days' journey away. Nevertheless, they all managed to get suitably sloshed.

It turned out that the tour group was Etienne's built-in fan club, cheering the triumphant capture of his Russian butterfly. He pulled out a handful of the newspaper clippings he had shared with them on the plane to Moscow.

Until that moment, I had no idea that he had used his contacts in the newspaper business to get several articles published about his seven-year struggle to marry the object of his adoration. All the articles were emblazoned with the headline, "Mon Amour Natasha," and photographs showed him dreamily staring at a framed picture of me.

The French ate it up like chocolate truffles. I was embarrassed beyond belief. When we got back to his home in Biarritz, were the city fathers going to give him a key to the city for successfully dragging me home to our marriage bed? I felt like a war trophy. What would life be like after this bizarre performance?

Technique

My favorite art teacher and longtime friend in Moscow was a petite dynamo, Anna Galanskova, whose well-appointed studio for teaching children was a resource for serious students. She had a huge collection of bottles, statues, skulls, and feathers, which we would arrange to create still-life paintings and sketches. I once spent the whole day in her studio, setting up objects and photographing them. "Still Life With Orange Bottle" is painted from one of these photos. For some reason, it always reminds me of the vodka-and-orange toasts Etienne's tour group made in the hotel in St. Petersburg.

I always work from a photograph when I do still life paintings that include glass objects, because when painting from life, the reflections change completely with the smallest shift of the light or the position of my body.

The main lessons to be learned from "Still Life With Orange Bottle" are about painting glass bottles and their reflections, and painting draped fabric. There are six glass objects in this piece—each a different color—making the painting a real challenge.

First, I studied each bottle in the photograph very carefully, identifying the white highlight that is usually the reflection of the light source. This highlight is clearly shaped and repeats the shape of the bottle. After outlining the outside edge of the bottle in clear resist, I outlined the main white highlight.

The most interesting step is to continue looking very attentively, studying all the remaining subtle and insignificant reflection shapes and drawing them on the silk with a soft pencil. In the case of the orange bottle, there was another important highlight shape, which I outlined with resist and then painted a light blue.

For the rest of the orange bottle, I painted a light yellow background. When it dried, I outlined all the remaining shapes with gutta resist on top of the yellow, making the gutta appear yellow. Then for the final layer of color, I used several different hues. Orange is dominant, but I also included blues, greens, and yellows, because the orange bottle reflects the other bottles as well as everything else that's close to it. I painted that layer with a very wet brush and sparingly applied a few salt crystals.

The key to painting folds in fabric—the other main element of the painting—is to understand clearly which geometrical shapes the folds create. Anyone can benefit from sketching folded, draped fabric whenever possible, because it helps to master the art of recognizing and drawing these shapes. By seeing each fold's underlying structure, I can sketch which side of it is illuminated, where I should indicate its shadowed side, and where the shadow that it casts should appear.

To paint the folds, I used some gutta, but relied more on the technique of applying soft shading at the perfect moment between wet and dry. The white fabric is surrounded by colored glass, and the colors in it reflect all the bottle colors, as well as the yellow wall. Using the appropriate reflected colors makes the fabric look even more realistic in the finished work.

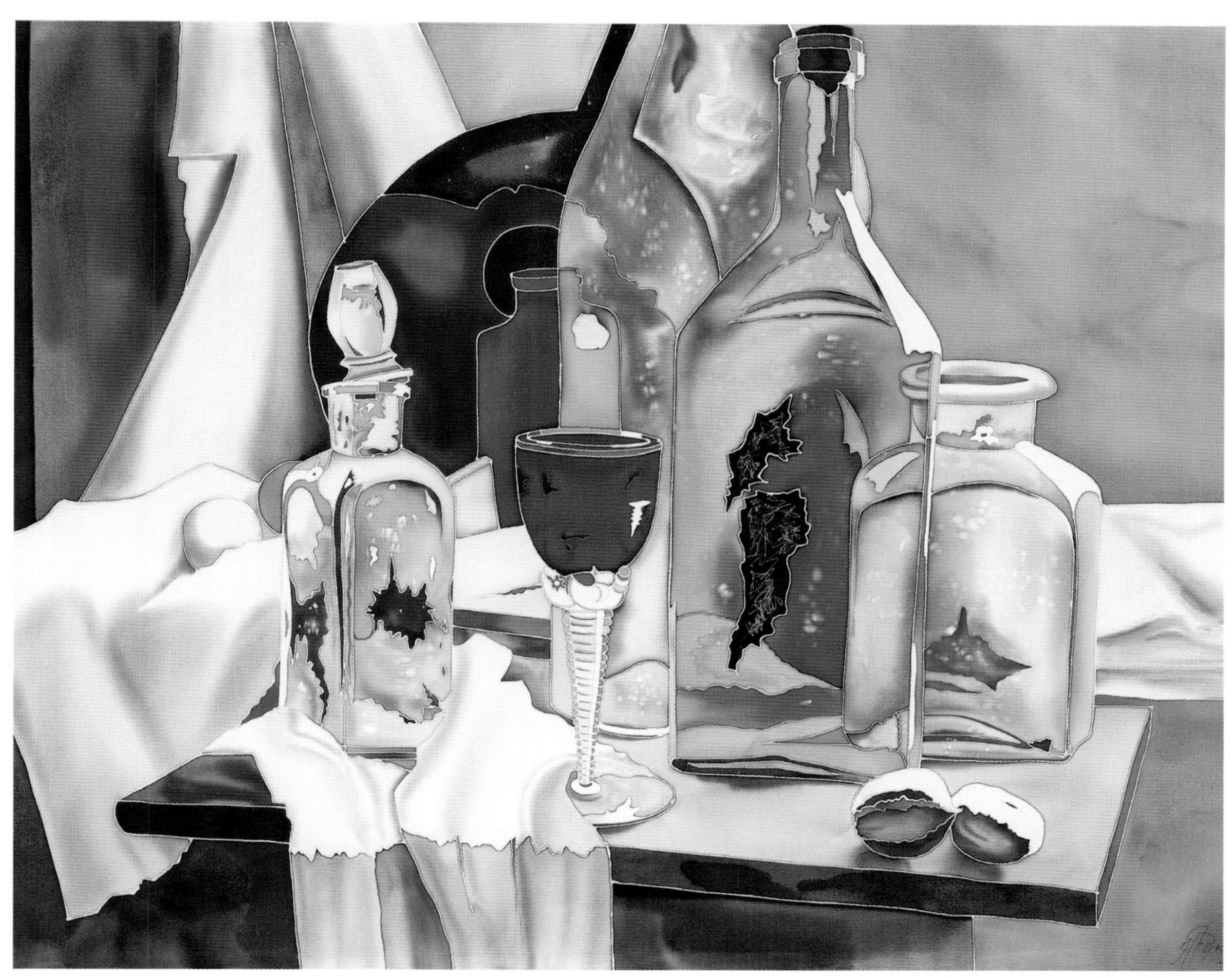

Still Life with Orange Bottle

11 France

Now I was married, with a stamp in my passport to prove it. But actually immigrating to France would require several years of navigation through the endless Soviet bureaucracy, so I made the necessary preparations to obtain a temporary visa.

Several committees grilled me on boring topics, like the history of the French Communist Party. How ironic! By consorting with a foreigner, I had just shown that I was morally flawed and a traitor, but now I had to prove I was politically correct enough to travel outside the Soviet Union.

I arrived at Orly airport outside Paris in the spring of 1985. Etienne met me, and drove me to exquisite Biarritz. A brilliant blue sky vibrated over cream-colored buildings, which were nestled around a rocky bay of pristine pocket beaches. Palaces and homes of the rich dotted the hills, and every house and garden was splashed with bougainvillea and poppies in neon reds and hot pinks. I couldn't wait to unpack and start painting.

Madame Cotard met us at the doorway of Etienne's modest home in a quiet working-class neighborhood, away from the glitzy hotels and beach-side nightclubs. But one glance at the little shepherdess figurines and frilly lamp shades in the front room brought me a devastating realization: neither of them had mentioned that Etienne lived with his mother. And it turned out that they both had plans for me that didn't include long sketching trips to the countryside. It was time to turn Natasha into a proper French housewife!

Etienne had a very definite idea of how a bed should be made. The freshly ironed sheets had to be drawn seventeen centimeters down across the pillows, and the foot of the bed had to be tucked in with military precision. Then there was cooking, which I had never really learned to do, since I had spent my teenage years studying for, and attending, art school. The first soufflé I served to my husband and his *maman* looked as if it had gotten third-degree burns just before it was flattened by a runaway bulldozer.

Madame Cotard was a caricature of the French upper-working-class woman, who hoped her attention to the fine details of housekeeping, marketing, cooking, and good manners would convey

that her family came from a better sort of people. She treated me like a little savage from the hinterlands, endlessly lecturing me on how to buy a good head of lettuce and avoid paying too much for it.

The shock of being in an utterly different culture began to sink in. For example, I was so sensually bombarded whenever I went into a French supermarket that I felt like I was under attack by heavy mortar. There were at least three hundred different types of cheese for sale. But when Etienne asked me what kind of cheese I wanted with the evening meal, I could merely mumble, because there were only two types of cheese for sale in Moscow—plain cheese and "Dutch" cheese. And neither was for sale in Biarritz.

Then there was the abundance of fresh vegetables. By contrast, if one of my Moscow neighbors had been lucky enough to find a cucumber in mid-winter, he would pass it around to the rest of us in the communal kitchen, so we could all inhale its wonderfully fresh cucumber smell and feel its green, glossy skin.

And then there were the rows and rows of cat and dog food. Some of the cans of gourmet pet treats looked like something people would queue up for in the snow in the Soviet Union, and be very glad to have. The comparison between these supermarket shelves, brimming with hundreds of different things to eat, and the struggles of my friends and family to put food on their tables year after year, was humiliating.

However, a discovery I made the first week I arrived in France gave me some satisfaction. I found a very old Russian church right in the middle of Biarritz, and met my first White Russian there—an aging Russian Orthodox priest—praying beside the banks of candles and glittering icons. He had immigrated to France to escape the Revolution and had, on the walls in his residence, several portraits of Czar Nicholas's family. He was the first person ever to tell me that Nicholas—and his wife and four children—had been murdered by the Bolsheviks. That piece of history had been eliminated, along with many other things, from Soviet history books.

Though I tried my best to adjust to French life, it was very difficult, despite the fact that I spoke reasonably good French. I had no way of knowing that of all the European countries, I had landed in the one where people looked right through you once they found out you weren't a native. And I felt that I could never be fully drawn into their world if I were merely tolerated. I took many weekend trips around southern France with Etienne and his mother, but I still felt like a tourist, even though I was married to a Frenchman.

At home, my training to be a good French wife continued. Madame Cotard even started buying what she considered proper clothes for me. They were either conservative little suits with matching shoes, or sweet floral-print dresses, tricked out in flowers and lace and ribbons.

The endless rounds of marketing and shopping and housecleaning kept me tired, and masked

the fact that I was becoming seriously depressed. With so much to learn, there was never enough time for painting or sketching. In part, I had come to France to experience freedom; instead, I had walked into a prison whose bars were much stronger and thicker than those of my "prison-like" existence in the Soviet Union.

To get some relief from my education as a proper human being, I asked to spend some time in the capital. Finally Paris—the unattainable dream of every Russian—would be mine!

I knew all about the artistic life of Montmartre, and had read the biographies of Van Gogh, Toulouse-Lautrec, and all the painters—Gaugin and Modigliani and Chagall. But I was shocked at the commercialization of Montmartre. Every sidewalk and street corner was crowded with vendors selling cheap knock-off paintings, or prints of "views of Paris." In Russia, art had never been reduced to a commodity. But in Montmartre, a half-dozen artists on every street corner offered to do your portrait. Mean-looking types with wraparound sunglasses and leather jackets, these Art Mafiosi would have probably snuffed you out if you had tried to draw on their turf.

Nevertheless, Paris was beautiful. Her architecture dazzled me for hours. Later on, Paris would give me much inspiration for my silk paintings. But emotionally, the city made me feel like a cork bobbing on the surface of the water, because she never wrapped me up and held me close to her breast, the way she had nurtured so many artists in the past. I felt shut out by the Parisians, who were interested only in themselves, and treated anyone with the misfortune to be born into another culture like an irrelevant, lower form of evolution—a sea slug or a beetle.

Back in Biarritz, I still found no time to paint or even sketch. Nor was I free to roam around the city alone, taking photographs as I had been doing everywhere since I was fourteen, because Etienne was jealous and controlling. Several times he said that if he let me out of the house alone, I would meet a nice art student on the street, be charmed by his good looks, and end up under the sheets with him.

It was unbelievably painful for me that he thought my bohemian life and sexy street clothes were fine for an art student, but now that I was a wife, I should act like one. My artistic life obviously meant nothing to him.

I began to have sleepless nights, reviewing the events of the previous few months, and found that things that I had erased from my daytime thoughts plagued my restless hours lying awake.

When we first came to Biarritz, Etienne and his mother had arranged a few parties, mostly for my husband's friends in the newspaper business, so that people could meet me. Nevertheless, the man and his busybody little mother seemed strangely isolated—especially when it came to their extended family, many of whom lived in the area.

Then I remembered that we had attended only one family gathering—organize so that everyone could meet the new bride. And one of Etienne's

cousins had drawn me out to the patio, where she kept asking how we were "doing." "Of course," she murmured hesitantly, "they've told you about his condition. . ."

But the only condition I knew about was my sorry housekeeping skills and bad cooking. So Monique explained that Etienne's skull had been slightly fractured during his forceps birth, and that he had suffered from intolerable headaches ever since, and was inclined to go into sudden rages.

No indeed, the "condition" had never been mentioned, nor had Etienne ever showed me the steel pin holding his skull together. But my heart started pounding as I remembered how, one afternoon, after I had made the bed incorrectly, he had taken me by the throat and shaken me with such tightly-clenched hands that I couldn't breathe.

As I lay awake each night, missing my mother, my country, and my art students, I realized that my dream of France, and of happily married life, had become a waking nightmare.

Technique

"Windswept" exemplifies the use of color, composition, and painting style to create a feeling—in this case, one of utter loneliness. Though I try to stay away from interpreting my own work, this painting clearly shows that I am leaving Paris as fast as I can.

Everything is muted and soft, as if underwater, and implies that it is beginning to rain. The sky colors are cold, and the darkness indicates that a big storm is coming. I sprinkled a few grains of ammonium salt on the trees to give the leaves the appearance of being tossed in the wind.

As a chemical engineer, my mother was interested in helping me find the perfect kind of salt for the effects I wanted to create. After I found that sodium chloride crystals made too hard and graphic an outline for my purposes, she brought home all kinds of salt from the lab for me to test. The best one was an ammonium salt—it comes from the lab in granulated form—which I crushed further to vary the size of the grains. When the salt hits a color mixed from several others, it chemically splits the mix to reveal some of the original hues, creating a rich visual effect that adds life to static shapes.

The curve of the fence and the street lead the viewer's eye deep into the painting, but the figure in the corner is hurrying away in the opposite direction, as if she is trying to disappear. And though the birds in the center give a certain feeling of contentment as they peck away at something on the street, they are not interested in the girl.

Painting trees and buildings involves learning how to eliminate most of the detail in a photograph. One must leave in just enough to make the meaning clear to the viewer. In real life, for example, the cathedral in the background is dripping with architectural detail, but I have included just the elements that are essential. And only a few of the leaves in the trees have been outlined in gutta; the rest have been created by the salt. As always, I created the green tones the best way: by avoiding the intense shades provided by the dye suppliers, and mixing my own.

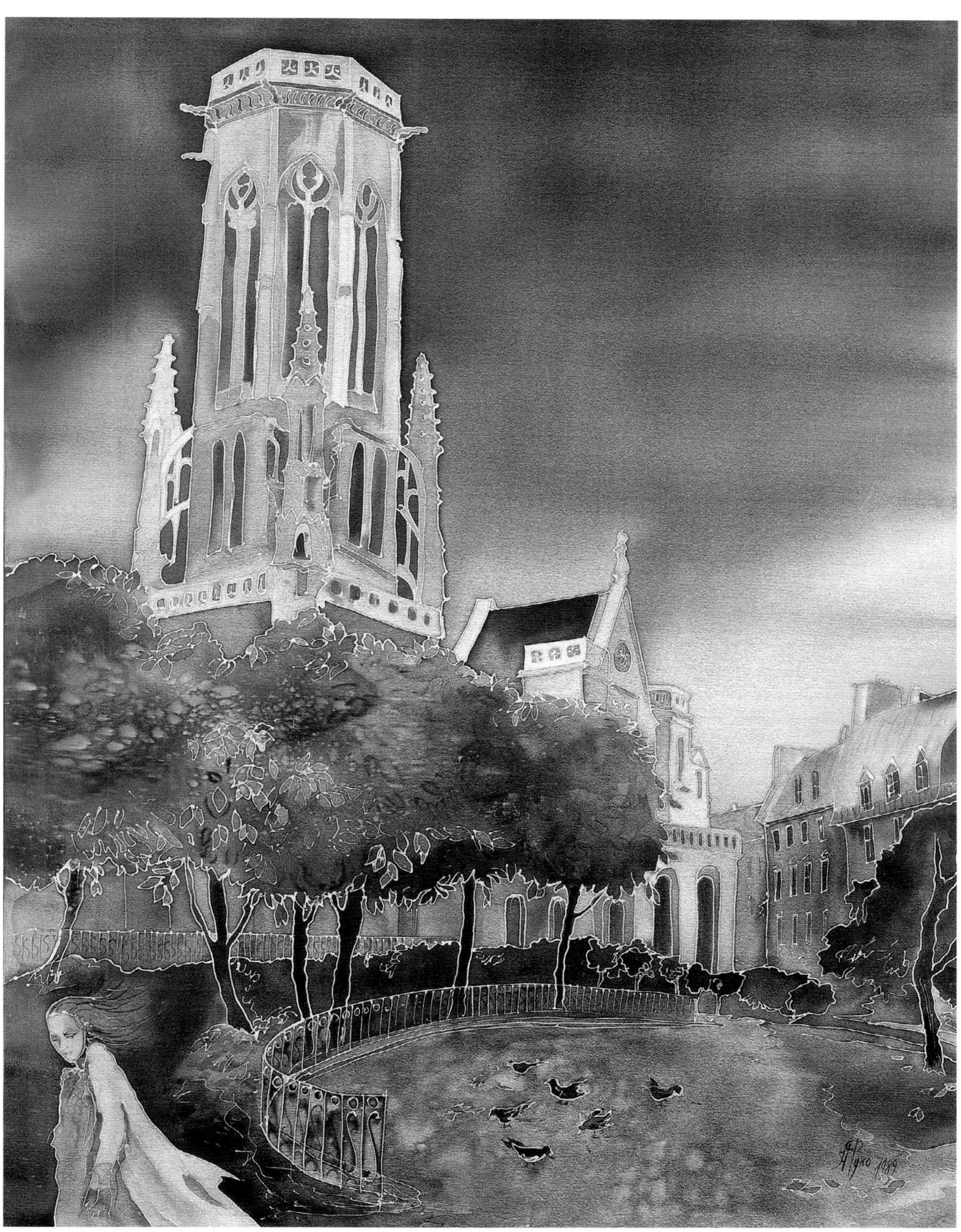

Windswept

...не быть не может
...те „Мадригала"
...ер...
...ью землетрясения,
...лчай Во всяком
у нас основательно

...л один, сов...
...ими дружи...
Зарек мо...
вообще не...
...е рассмотре...
наши рас...
...мне, мен...
он учит...
...то это он...
Наташи с...
...теорети...
...ись (ребенку меня)
...Пимена, и вырос...
...анатомией
...мая) импресси...
...же... и противно

...на редкость прекрасный
...Ринках вдохновенной
и ее мужем
...интересно. А из моих
...ции не признавал,
...а первая зевота у
...(хорошо в будни,
...дно единственная
...ствам не интересна,

...тра (симпатяга)

12 Swimming with Sharks

I risked one of Etienne's outbursts of rage by throwing a temper tantrum of my own, and it worked; I was given permission to walk by myself down to the beach to swim.

In some ways, Biarritz was the perfect place for me, because I love the water, and it was only a ten-minute walk to a spectacular beach of white sand dunes and dramatic rocky outcroppings. The craggy Bird Rocks, an exhilarating forty-minute swim past the breakers, provided a roost for flocks of sea birds and a goal for me. My daily swim to the Rocks gave me a sense of having accomplished something, a welcome change from the failure I felt like most of the time as a cook and housekeeper.

When they first noticed me swimming out to the Bird Rocks, the lifeguards lectured me about the strong undertow at the beach. And after quite an argument, they made me sign a form that released them from all responsibility for my safety. But I wasn't going to let some little detail like "endangering my life" keep me from doing the one thing that made my midsummer days tolerable, because I was otherwise caged up by a jealous husband in an airless little house.

One morning, as I ran my usual route to the beach, a woman in a big straw hat called out to me from the flower beds in front of her house. Sophie had met me at a party thrown by Etienne's journalist friends when I first came to Biarritz. We chatted for a while, and she invited me to visit whenever I wished. Her very un-French warmth and friendliness thawed me like warm water poured over cold hands. I explained that Etienne was not very sociable, and never let me out of his or his mother's sight except for my daily swim.

"You know, Natasha, we know what it's like for young women in Russia," Sophie replied, "and I want to be very frank with you. Life is very hard in your country. You meet this guy from France, and anyone would jump at the chance to have a better life in Europe. But there are ways you can get out of this. I work with Amnesty International, and we can help you stay here in France and get away from Etienne if you want to. Just tell me, and I'll talk to the right people."

Somehow, I didn't consider myself a candidate for an Amnesty International rescue. I could hardly be compared to the hundreds of political prisoners rotting away in remote Siberian prisons. What could she have seen in my face or behavior that conveyed my desperation? I told her I would think about it, but I didn't really take her offer seriously.

Several weeks later, I came to the beach much later than usual, and casually noticed that the tide was quite high. The strong swell sent waves crashing onto the usually dry rocks by the cliff stairway, and I could see that it was going to be very hard to get out past the breakers. I was standing knee-deep in the water, wondering if I should even try, when a man approached me and asked if he could join me. I didn't think that this short, trim guy could make it out to the rocks, and I told him so. He said he had watched me swim out the day before, and was sure he would succeed.

After several unsuccessful attempts, we made it past the breakers, breast-stroked out to the Bird Rocks, and sat there talking. He was a fascinating conversationalist—a journalist from Holland who spoke very good French—and I ate up the words of my attractive, dark-haired fellow swimmer like a starving refugee. I hadn't realized how lonely I was until I chattered in the sunshine with him for an hour, talking about anything and everything. My artist's eyes were fascinated by the way his blue ones reflected the ocean's color, with little flashes of gold radiating from the pupils.

Without warning, we were hit from behind by a wall of water. A huge wave broke over us, swept us off the rocks, and tossed us back up against them. Still unaware of the power of the high tide, we unsuccessfully tried to hold on to the rocks. But now we were covered with bloody cuts and scratches, because our skin was being torn to shreds by the mussel shells covering the rocks.

We decided that the only thing to do was swim for it. On the rough haul back, my grandmother's warnings suddenly popped into my thoughts. In Moscow, she always read magazine articles about sharks eating people in the Atlantic. And after my marriage, she had warned me never to swim in the ocean, because she knew how much I loved long-distance swimming. At the time, I thought it was hilarious. After all, I was planning to go to France, where my whole life would completely change, and Babushka was worrying about sharks. But swimming beside the journalist, I realized there was a distinct possibility that sharks would be attracted to the blood trailing from our scrapes and cuts. Several sharks had, in fact, been seen in the area recently. However, there was nothing to do but stroke as fast and hard as we could and hope that *Jaws: Beach at Biarritz* would not become the next box-office hit.

As soon as we got to the shore, a crowd surrounded us, having seen us struggling. Several people with cameras and a reporter from the local newspaper appeared, and they began taking notes and questioning us. The last thing I needed was to make the front page of the newspaper with a young male journalist beside me, covered with bleeding cuts. My husband's worst fears would be disastrously confirmed. So I ran home without saying goodbye to my companion.

Etienne was waiting at the front door, and my appearance triggered angry shouts. He shook me by my neck until I felt more like a dead rat than the half-drowned, bleeding one I already was. Then he ran off into the house, cursing me while he searched for bandages and ointment for my wounds.

After I was able to breathe again without pain, I made up a big story (though I never knew if he fell for it.) I said I had been sitting on the shore, and a big wave had swept me out and dragged me across the rocks.

Luckily, there was a bank robbery in Bayonne that same day, so my photograph never got into the newspaper. There's no telling what Etienne would have done if he had opened up his paper over his morning espresso and seen a picture of me standing on a crowded beach, covered with blood, under a headline that read, "Newspaperman's Wife and Dutch Journalist Narrowly Escape Death."

While I was recovering, I began to think about the dangerous things I had been doing. For example, about a month earlier, I had fallen from a borrowed motorcycle because I panicked and couldn't work the brake levers, and bashed my head pretty badly. Now I had a big scar on my forehead: the only doctor we could find on a Sunday evening to repair my wounds was a veterinarian who was used to the more practical job of stitching up dogs and cats. I had been recuperating for several weeks, and here I was again—coming home covered with blood and scratches.

Being bruised and in pain did, however, have one beneficial side effect; I was able to avoid making love with Etienne. He was not the world's greatest lover, and I had come to dread his unskilled attentions very soon after my arrival. Since the motorcycle accident, I had been able to put him off, and I knew my new set of wounds would give me a reprieve of several more weeks. He complained a lot about the situation, but there was nothing he could do about it.

I had read somewhere that when people feel trapped, they begin doing risky things as a way of crying for help. This psychological profile seemed to fit me well. I was severely depressed and feeling quite hopeless, and might have been suicidal if my background had been different.

A few weeks earlier, I'd heard Etienne and his mother discussing the suicide of a family member who had a good life, a nice husband, and her own car, but had been depressed for several months. I found this shocking. In the Soviet Union, I had never known anyone personally who committed suicide. Russian women are so overwhelmed trying to keep their lives together—standing in line for groceries, taking the children to day care and picking them up, and dealing with the endless cold of winter—that I don't think they have time to sit around getting depressed. Killing myself just wasn't an option.

I knew that Sophie could help me with her Amnesty International connections, but I had no way of contacting her and filling out papers—or whatever it took—without Etienne finding out. And I was tense and afraid because of his frequent rages and the memory of his fingers around my neck. So I slowly began to realize that I would return to Moscow when my six month's visa expired—no matter what anyone thought about it—and would never return to live with Etienne again. Somehow, I would extricate myself from this mess. I wanted my life back.

Two or three days after the big wave, I returned to the beach. As I came down the rough stone stairs cut in the cliff, the first person I saw was my swimming pal. I still didn't know his name, and we introduced ourselves. Franz looked pathetic. He had been forced to cut off his jeans at the knees, and rip apart his sandals, because his lower legs and feet were a mass of cuts. We talked about our accident over and over again. He left me his address, and I gave him my Moscow address and phone number. As a souvenir of our experience, he presented me with his swimming goggles. I had no way of knowing then that this was a major turning point in my life, and that my later friendship with Franz would have a huge effect on my silk-painting career.

My life *en famille* was an endlessly repeating cycle of the same routines, a way of life that my husband thrived on. Every weekend, Etienne and Madame Cotard and I would drive out to some little restaurant in the countryside, as French people all love to do—from the poorest to the richest.

Once settled in, we would spend at least a half an hour going over the menu. Every choice had to be discussed and debated, and the suitability of the wine had to be considered from every angle. It made me crazy with impatience.

But one day, I decided to bring along a sketch book. Maybe I could grab a few minutes to draw. After the hors d'oeuvres of *pâté de foie gras* and radishes dabbed with butter, I told Etienne and his mother that I wasn't that hungry, and wanted to go out for some fresh air.

The restaurant had a small garden with a stone arch that looked like a piece of ancient Roman architecture, and it probably was. I began to sketch, turning over page after page, filling my book. I felt more alive than I had in months: I was free again. But Madame Cotard's powdered little pink face suddenly appeared at the back door of the restaurant.

"Natasha, you have missed the best meal. My roast quail was heavenly, and Monsieur de la Ronde makes the best *tarte au poivres* in this whole region. You really should have stayed with us."

I could barely make myself respond politely, and apologized for my absence at the table. But this overbearing mother was not going to rule over me for much longer. I had begun to speak often about missing my own mother terribly and needing to visit her. In three weeks, my visa would expire, and I would be on the train back to Moscow—and painting again. I didn't care about the snow, the queues, or the lack of art supplies. I would be home.

Madame Cotard looked back toward Etienne with an exaggerated shrug. I didn't suppose she would ever understand, and I didn't care.

Memories of One Summer

Technique

Back in Moscow, I found that my frightening stay with Etienne had sapped my energy like a bad hangover. I painted every day to erase the unpleasant memories, and to reconnect with my former life and happier days.

Several summers previously, I had returned to Riga to visit my friend Marita. She was busy with ceramics classes, so I would take her daughter to the beach every day. That summer was hot and overcast, giving an unreal quality to the fog-enshrouded dunes by the sea.

I grouped several images for "Memories of One Summer," depicting the things I loved from that idyllic visit: Marita's red-and-white-checkered tablecloth; a ceramic bottle decorated with a geisha's image; a particularly ornate sea shell; Marita's red straw hat; and the little girl herself, standing in the warm, shallow water of the sea. The juxtaposition of unlikely objects, floating disconnectedly, makes this one of the most surreal of my paintings, especially with the contrast of the bright tablecloth against the murky colors of the sky.

I feel that if a painting is sincere—created from the emotions of the artist—it will touch the viewer's memories powerfully, and take on new meanings for them. The emotional charge is what makes one painting authentic, while another is just a technical exercise. For me, these images were a nourishing element of my healing process after the ordeal of living with Etienne. I always encourage other artists to paint what they care about, even if another set of images would do better at art shows and galleries. If you must create work because you know it will sell well, be sure to leave yourself time to create images that feed your soul.

13 Footloose

Genna and Losha met me at the train station in Moscow, laughing uproariously as they told me that Gorbachev's reforms included a national anti-drinking campaign. Gorby had ordered all the grapevines ripped up and burned in the Georgian vineyards, and every vodka distillery was turning out juice drinks and bottled water. With his typical Russian black humor, Genna announced that the people had invented a new drink in the face of this calamity—three squirts of cockroach killer into a home-brewed beer, as good as a shot of vodka. I was definitely home.

I returned to my familiar, cramped studio on Petrovka Street in the center of Moscow, with its paintings and art supplies stacked high around the narrow bed. Friends at parties, listening to my tales of Jekyll and Hyde in French clothes, understood my need to escape from Etienne's obsessive and controlling personality. But no one, especially my mother, wanted to advise me. She was afraid of recommending some plan and having it turn out badly.

However, the KGB contacted me soon after my return. Agent Yuri Vasilovich was the only one who had a definite idea about what I should do.

"You can't divorce him now," he purred. "We were just getting to know you. Besides, we want you to go back and report to us on the emigré artists in Paris. Come now, you'll have free travel, expenses paid, and be able to shop for whatever you want. Why would you turn down a nice life in Europe?"

My hand flew to my lips as I suppressed an ironic laugh by pretending to cough. How could I infiltrate the Russian emigré artists' community in Paris when my husband wouldn't let me out of his sight? I tried to explain to him about Etienne's personality and my virtual house arrest in Biarritz.

If I got a divorce from Etienne, my chances of leaving the Soviet Union again were minuscule. Only an invitation from my husband would get me back to France, and the KGB attention was unnerving. I felt confused and alone. Although I was somewhat aware that times were changing, I could never have foreseen the collapse of the Soviet Union and the loosening of travel restrictions after 1991, five years later.

Seeing France through the window of Etienne's car had been duller than televised reruns of Communist Party speeches. I daydreamed about traveling freely, on my own terms, like the old days of Riga and Prague. When I received Etienne's second invitation to visit him, I came up with the perfect solution. I would use the requisite invitation to get a visa to France without telling my husband, and mark on my map a one-hundred-mile danger zone around Biarritz. He didn't need to know that I intended to leave him permanently.

Standing in line for my train ticket to Paris, I overheard a conversation about special round-trip ticket from Paris to any point in France that allowed one to stop as often as one wanted at no extra charge. Impulsively, I bought a round-trip ticket from Paris to Nice. I would see the French Riviera, take photographs, and sketch, bringing oceans of blues and pinks and greens into my paintings, as well as the classical Roman ruins that reflected the golden light of Provence.

When I first arrived in Paris, I stayed in the apartment of one of the French girls I had met when they were studying Russian in Moscow. But Catherine's constant fights with her Russian boyfriend in Paris soured our relationship, and one night I was locked out of her tiny garret with nowhere to go.

I pulled out my address book and scanned it quickly by the telephone in the Metro station. Olga, a Russian woman who had married a wealthy Parisian businessman, was my best bet. Her daughters had taken art classes from me during a Moscow visit the year before, and she had given me her phone number in Paris, with the usual polite words to call her if I ever needed anything.

Luckily, Olga was still awake, and said I could come over and spend the night. The next morning, I explained how the situation with Catherine had deteriorated, and told her I was looking for a place to stay for the two months until my visa expired.

Olga offered to let me stay and be a nanny to her two daughters. She lived in a palatial apartment on Avenue Wagram near the Arc de Triomphe. And through her, I learned about the social behavior of Russians who lived in Paris. In order to withstand the snubs of the exclusive Parisians, Olga and her friends had become snootier, fighting unfriendliness by meeting it with an even more dramatic level of disdain. They didn't even seem to like each other. It was very bizarre.

One afternoon, after shopping for an affordable bathing suit at a discount store in a bad neighborhood, I had all my money stolen from my purse, the two thousand francs of foreign currency I had been allowed to take out of the Soviet Union. In order to have some money to live on, I gave some silk-painting classes, and sold some of my favorite hand-painted silk garments for a fraction of their worth.

One of Catherine's art student friends, Odile, was from Nice. And before my friendship to Catherine had cooled, Odile had invited me to come and stay with her the last week of August.

When I told Olga about my previously purchased train ticket to Nice, she argued about my leaving. Though she was quite wealthy, she wasn't about to give up her free child care without a struggle. I pleaded with her, saying that I had bought the ticket in Moscow in rubles, and that I couldn't afford to waste this chance to travel cheaply to a part of the world I might never see again. Finally, she relented. I didn't dare tell her I only had fifty francs to my name.

I clmbed on the train at the Gare du Nord, my backpack stuffed full with a change of clothes, my camera, the now not-so-cheap bathing suit, and a bottle of wine. It had been a cold and rainy summer in Paris, so I was wearing boots and a leather jacket.

I doubted that Odile would meet me at the train station in Nice, because she was only a casual acquaintance, and our arrangement had been scribbled on the back of a cafe bill one evening in the Rue de Flores. But to my relief and delight, she was there to welcome me.

At a restaurant later that evening with her art school friends, she excitedly told me about her parents' house in a beautiful fourteenth-century village in the French Alps. Inspired by the opportunity to show her home to a Russian visitor, she decided to drive me there immediately.

I was drunk from the wine and the wild freedom of these young people, driving through the warm, lavender-scented Provençal night in a yellow convertible sports car. I clutched the door frame as we took the crazy hairpin turns of the mountain road—sure I was going to die, but die happy. We spent four great days in the mountains, exploring all the villages. Houses and bridges built of ancient stone hung in clefts of the mountains like eagles' nests.

After I returned to Nice, I stayed at the home of Odile's friend, Patrick, and it became my home base for several unbelievably frenzied day trips. I was finally in the France of my dreams, and I was going to squeeze in as much of it as one human being could.

Rousting myself at four one morning, I took a dawn train to Monte Carlo. How could I not visit fabled Monaco, where Dostoevsky's gambler, Protkin, had lost his family's fortune? Had they bothered to look up on the way to their limos, the jewelry-draped patrons gliding out of the casino after a night of expensive fun would have seen a wild-haired, ecstatic woman gaping at the elegant front entrance in her boots and leather jacket, snapping photos of the gilded Corinthian columns. I felt like yelling to them: "Hey, it's me, Natasha—I'm in Monte bloody Carlo!"

Russian authors, from Pushkin to Lermontov, have described Menton, the spa town in the south of France where the wealthy Russian nobility traveled to take the mineral waters. So after a few hours in Monte Carlo, I took the train to see for myself. In Menton, I climbed my way up through the narrow stone streets to a cemetery perched dizzily at the top of the town; its three-tiered terraces of slanting gravestones reflected Menton's layers of culture: French, Italian, and Russian. I sat in the cemetery, my back against a fellow Russian's elaborately carved stone, sipping from my bottle of wine and inhaling the view. I sketched the layers and layers of buildings and churches, and in the distance, the yachts dancing against the brilliant blues of sea and sky. Life couldn't get any better!

My French was pretty good by then, and I could communicate well enough with the people I met. They could never guess where I was from, having never seen tourists from the Soviet Union, and I had great fun with their confusion.

Back at Patrick's place in Nice, sharing my adventures with him and his girlfriend in the evening, I would prepare a cup of instant beef bouillon for dinner. I pretended that I always drank it for my health. Actually, I was making my fifty francs last the whole trip, but Patrick and Sylvie would never know. They were convinced I couldn't live without the salty brown cubes.

It was time for my last marathon day trip. The first stop on the train from Nice back to Paris was Antibes, the exquisite Côte d'Azur resort where Picasso had painted, and now the home of the first museum dedicated to his work. I got off the train, took in the museum, jumped back on another train, and got off again at Cannes. I walked along the Promenade Anglais, where all the action takes place during the Cannes Film Festival, and trudged several miles to Old Cannes, with its ornate mansions and gardens.

Marseilles was a much bigger city, however, and I overestimated my strength searching for a famous Baroque church in the scorching heat of the Provençal sun. I flopped down onto a bench to take a rest, lost somewhere in the Old Port area. Then, as I always do, I handed my camera to some strangers and asked them to take my picture. I had stripped down to my bathing-suit top and jeans, but not wanting to look too undressed in the photo, I slipped my leather jacket over my shoulders. Later, reviewing my photos from the journey, I saw that I looked like a semi-retired seventies rock star who had taken one trip too many.

When I visited Marseilles years later and recounted my adventures, my friends scolded me

for wandering around alone and for trusting strangers to return my camera. The Old Port had a deadly reputation, because half the drugs in Europe were then funneled through its narrow, seedy streets; my friends told me I was lucky I hadn't been sold into white slavery. But I had been oblivious—elated and exhausted at the same time.

I threw all my things on a rocky, narrow strand near the fishing boats and took a swim. My heels were so blistered that I could barely walk. As I devoured some chocolate cookies, I realized that my precious fifty francs were all spent, and reluctantly decided to return to Paris.

The fast TGV train from Marseilles to Paris seemed to be flying, and the smooth ride put me to sleep immediately. When I woke up just an hour later, the conductor was announcing Avignon. Avignon! I just couldn't miss out on seeing the Pope's palace and Van Gogh's haunts! Half asleep, I staggered off the train.

It was toward evening, around seven or eight, when I limped slowly around the magnificent palace before collapsing on the stone pavement to eat the last crumbs of my cookies. But then, from my resting place, I could see sculptures in a garden—a great subject for a future painting—at the very top of the palace grounds. After a painful climb, I was sitting next to the garden's iron gates, disappointed at finding them shut and locked for the evening. But a young couple from East Germany joined me, and we shared stories about our travel adventures. Emboldened by the good company, we climbed over the iron gates and took pictures of each other laughing among the sculptures.

Brigit and Rohan drove me all over Avignon in their old Volkswagon bus, pointing out all the great buildings and Roman ruins. Some time after midnight, they put me back on the TGV. When I pulled out my battered ticket, which was more holes than ticket by now, the conductors had quite a time trying to figure out how I had gotten to so many parts of France on a single round-trip ticket. Finally one old fellow solved the dilemma with his map: I had gone through Brest—a Soviet city on the Polish border—not the town of Brest on the rocky coast of Brittany in northwestern France. Their earnest faces were more than I could bear in my exhaustion, and I dissolved into gales of silly laughter, then fell asleep sitting up.

A Russian friend was waiting for me at the Gare du Nord in Paris when the TGV pulled in at dawn. "What ever is wrong with your feet?" he asked.

I was mincing painfully along the platform in my leather boots with my toes pointing toward the sky like a circus clown. Upon closer inspection, we discovered that the heels of my boots—not just the replaceable first layer, but the entire heel—had completely disappeared. I had been too tired to notice.

Technique

While I was staying in Paris at Olga's, the family was invited to dinner at the extravagantly gilded palace of an old noble French family near the Bois du Boulogne. As the nanny, I was allowed to tag along. After dinner, I wandered off into the kitchen with my camera, and found a carafe of water and some silverware drying on a napkin. Later, when I examined my slides of the trip, I realized how beautiful the water in the carafe was as it reflected the silver. The pattern it created made the water seem alive—moving with its own energy.

From this slide, I painted my first still life on silk. Until then, I had only painted landscapes on silk.

Though my still lifes since then may be better technically, I still feel this painting is my best, because I really captured the water and reflections. It is also the painting that began my journey of discovering beauty in unexpected places. The usual notion of beauty—a vase of roses or a sunny garden—had never fired my imagination. For me, the best still lifes are the natural ones, not the ones I've set up purposefully. In "Water and Silver," I intensified my lifelong fascination with water and reflections in glass.

Water and Silver

14 Holland & Belgium

Of course, my running away from Etienne had its consequences. His phone calls came in waves—three or four during one week, then silence for the next two months. Each time he called and asked when I was coming back, I would make excuses: I was having trouble getting a visa; I really missed my mother and Russia when I was in France; I had a silk-painting commission that I had to finish. Finally, after an angry tirade from Etienne during a midnight call, I stammered that I might never come back if he was going to behave that way—his rages frightened me too much. This set him off even worse. He shouted, "Don't worry—you will come back, do you hear me, *you will come back!*" Too upset to talk any more, I just told him I'd work on it, and hung up.

Several weeks after that disturbing exchange, I received a much more reassuring call from Franz, one which took me quite by surprise. I must have made a strong impression on my Dutch journalist friend on that day, six months previously, when we were washed off the rocks together in Biarritz. He was flying to Moscow to cover a high-powered meeting between the Soviet defense ministries and those of several European countries. Would I like to show him the sights and be treated to a few dinners? He would only be in the city for five days.

Once we were together again, our conversations flowed as effortlessly as they had during those hours we spent on the Bird Rocks. Franz could make anything funny, and his ironic sense of humor added spice to our visits to Red Square, St. Basil's Cathedral, and Donskoi Monastery.

The days flew by quickly, and I told him I wanted to give him a small thank-you gift for the delicious dinners in restaurants only foreigners and Party members could afford. His schedule was very tight, so he asked me to meet him outside the wrought iron gates of the Ministry of Defense.

Franz slipped out of a courtyard packed with soldiers flashing every conceivable weapon. They looked like bulldogs with their studded collars. Dark-suited operatives just inside the fence watched us closely, blatantly listening to everything we said. I felt as if I were in a Russian spy movie as a key agent is being transferred to a safe house to take on her new identity. As we hugged goodbye, I quickly passed him the small box containing my gift, a Russian-made watch. Later, riding home on the Metro, I was sure that guards would arrest me at every station.

The following spring, Franz called from Brussels, where he was covering the European Parliament. After our companionable times, it was easy for me to accept his invitation to visit him in Belgium. This slightly-built man, with his intelligence, grace, and mischievous green eyes, could charm the socks off a snake.

Franz called the Belgian Embassy and asked if there were any way the usual six weeks' waiting period for a visa could be shortened. The clerk replied that the only exceptions were for dead bodies: you could get a corpse through in one week.

"Well, if we have to kill Natasha to get her here faster, we'll have to do it, but you must know that I'd really prefer her alive. . ."

Getting a low-level Belgian Embassy clerk to laugh is like blowing hard on a frozen lake to make it melt. But Franz was rewarded by a little chuckle. His conversation must have caused a slight thaw at the embassy, because my visa was ready a week later. I tried to add Holland to the visa so that

I could visit Franz's father, but that was impossible without a separate application, and the Soviet passport agency warned me not to violate the terms of my visa by crossing additional borders. If I did that, they wouldn't allow me out of the country again, and I didn't want to lose the opportunity to continue taking advantage of the increasingly looser Soviet restrictions on foreign travel.

Franz met my train in Brussels and announced that he had to change his plans. I thought he said, "I have to see my Papa in Strasbourg," and I was confused, because I knew his father lived in Holland, and there was no way I could go to France.

"No no, not my Papa, I have to cover a big meeting attended by the Pope. Don't worry about the borders—I'll talk my way through and you'll be fine."

I was very tired from the two-day train ride and promptly fell asleep in the car. When I awoke, we were already in France, having passed through the borders of Belgium and Luxembourg without a hitch. Franz saw my eyes widen with anxiety and joked that he had told the border guards I was dead and they had just waved us through. As he put it, "Being dead seems to make a better impression on all these government officials. . ."

Representatives from sixteen European countries were meeting in Strasbourg to discuss the economic unification of Europe. Every journalist worth their salt was in the huge press room, calling their home offices, typing into computers, and dashing about expectantly as they waited for the Pope. Franz introduced me to them as his assistant.

Suddenly, a whirlwind of agitation and movement announced the Pope's arrival. There he was, in his white robes, smiling and shaking our hands. I felt so important meeting him!

For several weeks, I traveled all over Holland, Luxembourg and Belgium, following the trail of Franz's work assignments. In that way, I saw much more than the usual tourist did, and had plenty of time to take pictures in ancient little Belgian towns like Bruges and Ghent, with their canals, carved bridges, and picturesque churches.

At some point on these trips, we became lovers. This happened easily and naturally, for Franz was the first man in my life with whom romance was fun. He laughed as readily in bed as he did when he was fully dressed. Making love was simply an extension of the warmth and ease we felt with each other, and was as effortless as eating or breathing. Franz just wouldn't take anything seriously. He was a complete contrast to any man I had been involved with before.

Every time we were about to cross into a different country, he would warn me that the border was coming up and I should prepare myself. I would sit stiffly in my seat, nervously chewing on my nails as any Russian person would, and a few miles later, I would ask him if we were at the border yet.

"Oh, sorry," he'd laugh, "that was Belgium back there on the other side of the river. This is Holland."

Amsterdam's wild atmosphere made beer-splashed Prague seem like a maiden aunt's formal tea; and Moscow, a year-long funeral. The weather was unusually sunny and warm that year, and freedom filled the air with a perfume as strong and sweet as the marijuana smoke that lay in a haze outside the cafes and bars. Waiters would bring a lunch menu to our table along with a small hand-lettered scrap of paper that listed the drug specials of the day. I strolled wide-eyed through the notorious red-light district, with its prostitutes offering their services in display windows.

I had brought two dozen of my silk paintings with me, though I felt only the slightest hope of selling any of them. I had stripped them from their frames and rolled them up in my suitcase to avoid the hefty fee extracted by the Soviet Ministry of Culture for bringing "treasures of the country" across our borders. Ironically, I had never exhibited any of these "treasures" at home. Each city had its own powerful Artists' Union, and getting into it involved a discouraging round of filling out forms, standing in long lines clutching your work, and—for most people—getting rejected. Too many of my friends had been humiliated by the words, "This is not art. It's garbage." And we couldn't even buy art supplies without being a member of the Union, let alone exhibit our work.

I had a particular problem, since painting on silk didn't fall neatly into any of the four rigid Artists' Union categories of oil, sculpture, decorative art, and graphics. The officials told me to paint on paper, so I could be pigeonholed into the graphics category with the watercolor and pastel artists. It was very discouraging, but I had found the perfect medium for my work and was not going to change for these old bureaucrats, wrapped like mummies in their stifling views of what was art and what wasn't.

On the days that Franz worked, I kept myself busy reframing my paintings. My carpentry skills were a joke and the frames were wretchedly crooked and weak.

Several times Franz had stumbled over the growing stack in his apartment's entryway. One day he asked, "Do you want to have an exhibit, or a show, or something?" as he dashed off to do an interview.

I had no idea how that could be done, but Franz did. He called a journalist friend who covered the arts, and they found an exhibit space for me in Breda. I had to be ready in two days. I leaped around the room, laughing insanely. This was something incredible—my first show!

Franz's editor-in-chief interviewed me for an article that would come out in the Breda newspaper the same day as my opening. We hung my work in a small section of the gallery where an established Dutch artist was having an opening the same night.

Franz invited all his friends, and the crowd for the Dutch artist made it a big event. I was still a novelty then—a Russian artist—and was surrounded with friendly Dutch people asking me questions about life in the Soviet Union and about my work. I got really nervous and downed many glasses of wine offered by friendly hands. By the end of the show, I had sold eight paintings, and I was wild with happiness!

We went off to a bar to celebrate. This journalists' hangout had two hundred types of beer, and I was giddily trying to taste half of them. One of Franz's colleagues who had bought two of my paintings accused me of not being Russian, because I wasn't drinking vodka. It was an insult not to be taken lightly by any red-blooded Russian, so I ordered a glass of vodka and swallowed it in one gulp. Everyone expected me to fall over, but nothing happened. Loud cheers followed us as we left the bar to go to dinner at the home of Franz's editor.

By the time Dirk's wife and daughter had served the cassoulet, I was stone drunk. I spoke Russian whether anyone understood me or not, English with French-speaking Catherine, French with English-speaking Franz, and a dizzy combination of all three as the evening unfolded. Several glasses of wine into the meal, I flopped over and fell asleep with my head on the table. I still cringe with embarrassment at how recklessly I drank that night, flush with my first success.

The next morning in Franz's apartment, I saw the Breda newspaper on the kitchen table and asked Franz to translate my article.

"Don't you remember?" he laughed. "We translated it for you at dinner in all the languages you know!"

But I didn't remember anything after the vodka. During the rest of my stay in Holland, Franz arranged several more exhibits for me, and I sold more paintings. But I learned to drink less each time I celebrated.

I was eager to return to Moscow and build on this burst of creative energy, happiness and financial well-being. As the weeks had unfolded, I realized that Franz had fallen in love with me in

Biarritz. But my love for him was better defined as a profound appreciation of a wonderful human being. Franz was looking for someone to settle down with, to continue as his companion and assistant on his work assignments; he could tell that I wasn't of a nature to shape my life to another person's. My desire for crazy adventures and the life of the freewheeling artist was still stronger than anything else in my being, including the urge for romantic connection. And I was still traumatized by my frightening captivity with the abusive Etienne. Franz and I parted as friends, and lifelong friends we remain.

Technique

"Holland, Canal Scene" is another painting that celebrates my love of reflections. Like St. Petersburg and Venice, the architecturally rich city of Amsterdam, ribboned with canals, affords me infinite possibilities for subject matter. For this piece, the windows in the tall buildings across the canal offered me the chance to create a second and third layer of reality—what was inside the buildings, and what was reflected from behind my viewpoint.

To paint reflections in water successfully, I must first study my photographs at length to see what is reflected, how it is distorted, and how the colors break up and jump across each other. Often I will take one shot with the buildings in focus, and another that focuses on the reflections. If the reflection is too still, the painting will confuse the viewer, so I soften it by reducing the amount of detail, blending the colors, and applying salt. I have found that I can reduce the amount of detail, but never add detail: for some reason, the additions always look false.

For the first time, brilliant tomato red appears in one of my paintings; here, it is on the prominent central rectangle of the canal boat's cabin. In Holland and Belgium I was enjoying my own freedom, and Amsterdam's wild lifestyle certainly affected my experience there. The red reflects the vibrant, passionate energy I felt, as well as my new confidence as a professional artist.

Holland, Canal Scene

15 The Blue Volvo

With the money I made on my silk paintings, I was able to make arrangements to buy a car. I couldn't come close to affording one in Russia, where car loans just didn't exist. With my own transportation, I wouldn't have to depend on friends to help me haul around my increasingly big and unwieldy paintings.

My friend Misha, the attorney who wrote the poem about my apple orchard painting, had given me the name of a somewhat shady Russian used car dealer in the dirty industrial port city of Antwerp. Alex, the dealer, showed me a few ugly Russian Ladas, but I couldn't take my eyes off a gorgeous dark blue Volvo sedan with worn leather upholstery, only eight years old, that had a huge trailer hook at the back. I was a very bad driver, and I figured that other drivers would avoid rear-ending me when they imagined my trailer hook tearing a big hole in their radiators.

Since the Volvo cost the same as the old Russian cars—about two thousand dollars—I handed Alex my precious wad of cash. He had some deal with the port that allowed him to ship the car cheaply for another five hundred. The Volvo would be shipped to Riga, and I would have to pick it up there. So I left Belgium with the ownership papers stuffed in my purse.

Back in Moscow, I kept telephoning Alex, but still no car. He couldn't arrange for space on a ship, he said, and made so many excuses that I thought I would never see my car or my money again. Etienne kept calling from Biarritz, demanding to know when I would return, but I just kept telling him I needed time to think about it.

A year later, Alex called me to say, "Tomorrow I am shipping your car. Be in Riga in two days."

For the trip to Riga, Misha loaned me his car and an employee, Sergei, who was an excellent driver. And I towed along my sort-of boyfriend, Yuri, who knew about foreign cars from working as a driver in Moscow.

We arrived in Riga on a Thursday evening. All my friends had told me that we should meet the car at the docks ourselves or it would be stripped bare by a gang of toughs.

We tried to enter the port at the gatehouse, but the guard just laughed. "You must be kidding!

You'll need papers signed by five different ministries and it's Thursday. Friday, no one works. So just come back on Monday. We'll keep your car here, don't worry. . ."

Sergei had to get Misha's car back to Moscow by Monday, and he couldn't possibly hang around in Riga until then. So Yuri and I snuck around to a part of the fence where the guards couldn't see us, and climbed over the barrier, which was topped with barbed wire. Sergei threw some canned food over the fence after us in case we got locked in for days and got hungry. Then Yuri and I ran to the area where two foreign cars had been delivered, and spotted a bunch of thugs who had started to unscrew everything that could be removed from my Volvo. Regular infusions of cash evidently made the guards miraculously blind to these busy dismantlers.

When we approached, waving my ownership papers, they melted into the twilight. They had already taken the radio and the headlights, and the locks were broken, but we had my car. We camped out on the worn leather upholstery of the Volvo and ate from the cans of food until Monday morning.

After making all the rounds to get my papers signed, we drove off, and spent the night in the Volvo somewhere in the dense pine forests of Latvia. The next morning, as we drove along the desolate two-lane highway in Belarus, a car materialized in our rear view mirror: five men stuffed in a Lada with Abkasian license plates.

Every Muscovite had heard that bandits from this tiny, mountainous republic on the Black Sea had been killing isolated travelers just to steal their cars. Raw fear pulsed a stabbing pain through my gut. What a silly mistake I had made! There were only about four Volvos in Moscow at the time, and my elegant foreign car would attract trouble like a beautiful blonde alone in a bar.

Yuri nervously chain-smoked while the Abkasians tailed us for three hours. We hoped to find safety at a village soon, but we were almost out of gas. As my boyfriend turned into a little gas station along the highway, he checked the rear view mirror to see if the other car would follow—and smashed head-on into the concrete platform holding the gas pumps.

I began to cry as the five men got out of their car and silently walked around my damaged Volvo. They might have towed it with a rope, but the front axle was bent. So the mute Abkasians piled back into their Lada and drove off. We were convinced that we had just escaped being murdered, and that Yuri's accident had probably saved our lives.

Several hours later, a truck driver showed up to claim the double-trailer semi that was parked at the gas station. He was going to Moscow with one trailer full, and would haul my Volvo in the empty trailer for the rest of the money Yuri was carrying. It took us three more days to locate a crane operator to lift the car into the trailer. It was mid-week, but all the operators in that desolate, rural region were already drunk. A pickled local arrived with his crane and hooked the Volvo in four places. We watched, gritting our teeth, as two of the hooks fell off the crippled vehicle and left it dangling upside down in mid-air. *This was going to be my first and last car,* I thought.

Somehow the crane operator still managed to load the car, and we made the rest of the trip in the cab with the truck driver, at a bone-rattling twenty kilometers an hour over badly paved highways. Yuri felt guilty about the wreck, and helped me get my car repaired.

Back in Moscow again, Misha had quit his job as a poorly-paid chief prosecutor. Only bribes kept most of the government lawyers like him out of near poverty, and he refused to take them. I was a bad influence, I suppose, because I'd convinced him to work for a private investigative law firm, and his new job involved meetings with some of the most powerful men in the Russian Mafia. The chief Mafia boss in Moscow at that time, known to all as "the Professor," had a blue Volvo, and Misha always borrowed my blue twin to impress him.

I nearly got killed a second time in this car as well, when Misha and I foolishly confronted

some gun-toting thieves we'd caught in the act of stealing my hubcaps. Misha began calling the Volvo "Natasha's crime magnet." Two years later, I bought a really beat-up-looking Lada that attracted no particular attention, making it the safest thing on the road.

But my troublesome car had opened the door to an artistically rich and productive phase of my life that in some ways has never been surpassed. With transportation to get out of town, I would travel to the countryside on my own, whenever and wherever I wanted. Although I can be very outgoing, and love to socialize with friends, the nature of my artwork requires long stretches of uninterrupted solitude. When friends drop in without warning and the phone rings constantly, I cannot work well.

By this time, my grandmother on my mother's side had moved back in with her daughter, and I had to move into *babushka's* two-room apartment on Vichnevskovo Street in a bleak, worn-out neighborhood far from the city center. Although I didn't know it at the time, my mother had engineered this move, hoping that the privacy would encourage me to have boyfriends, get married, and make some babies.

Anybody in Moscow would have jumped at the chance to have a two-room place all to themselves. There were plenty of families of six or eight people living in cramped spaces, with the added annoyance of a communal kitchen and bath. My kitchen was only eight feet square, and decorated with my grandmother's favorite motif: white polka dots on a red background. But it was luxuriously all mine.

However, there was something about her apartment that felt really creepy. Was it her heavy old furniture and faded drapes? Or had something terrible happened there in the past? Moreover, there were several floors of people above me—an arrangement that always depresses me. I never told anyone, since they would have thought I was crazy, but I hated that apartment.

My blue Volvo took me to a hundred picturesque places in the surrounding countryside. The next three summers after returning from Holland, I rented an attic room in a dacha in the village of Troitskoe, right beside the Moscow-Volga Canal, with a beautiful view overlooking meadows and forest. The cool waterway, as wide as a lake, would beckon me every morning, and I would plunge in for a long swim. Since I am happiest when no one lives above me, and when I live a stone's throw from water I can swim in, my summer dacha rental was my personal version of heaven on earth.

The dacha I rented in the winter nestled in the famous writers' village of Peredelkino, where Boris Pasternak lived and wrote and is buried. Persecuted by the Soviet authorities for writing works like Doctor Zhivago, he was forced to return his Nobel Prize and was expelled from the Writers' Union. The village was still a refuge for writers like Bulat Okudjava, a popular contemporary Russian poet and singer.

I loved the feeling of the literary surroundings, but no one really knew me there, and I kept it that way. The solitude was exactly what I needed.

Even after I learned to drive in the snow, my trips to Peredelkino were a one-woman comedy act. But luckily, there were very few other vehicles on the road in the winter. The Volvo's tires were completely bald, and I would half drive, half skid down the road, bashing into the huge snowbanks on either side. And getting the Volvo in and out of the dacha's gates was a constant struggle. The snow would fall several feet at a time, and a friendly neighbor, Vasily, had to help me with the endless shoveling.

I would leave Moscow with one or two weeks' provisions—a couple of chickens to make a big pot of soup, a bag of potatoes, plenty of tea, jars of pickled cabbage, and a bottle of vodka. The dacha was actually heated in winter, since the village had once been a haven for privileged Writers' Union members, and a big snow bank served as my refrigerator.

Ensconced in a wide, veranda-like room with floor-to-ceiling paned windows, I looked out on the snow-filled garden, sipping my tea and watching fiery orange sunsets through the bare branches of the trees. In the distance, the sweet, sad moan of a train's whistle floated across the silent fields. Ideas for new pieces appeared in my mind's eye faster than I could capture them on paper, but I was still completing a painting every day.

Snoring loudly, a hugely fat orange cat, Marquise, sprawled on a braided rug in front of the tiled stove. When the owner of the dacha rented the three rooms to me, he had said, "There's an animal there. He comes with the dacha."

I had never had a cat before, and fell in love with Marquise. He crept unplanned into many paintings. I talked to him like a person during the gloomy winter days and nights. The big clown was so bold that he would try to take the food off the fork on its way to my mouth. Besides what I gave him, Marquise visited three or four other dachas and sat outside, meowing for hours. Each owner thought poor Marquise was neglected, and fed him. After working the neighborhood for handouts, the orange beggar—growing larger by the day—would come back to me through the open top of the kitchen window, and a loud thud would announce his arrival.

But I wasn't the only girl in love with him. Neighbors' female cats would prowl around on the roof at night and yowl in pleading tones, calling him out for an amorous rendezvous. He would slowly get up and haul his huge body out the window, as if the extra effort was almost too much for him to bear. The indolent Marquise ruled the neighborhood like the French noble for whom he was named. We were all his loyal subjects.

Friends wondered if I was afraid to stay alone at the dacha in winter. There may have been some danger from petty thieves, but I was so immersed in my painting, and so nourished by the peace and stillness and beauty, that I just wasn't thinking about the outside world and its problems. To me, it was the true life of the artist, and I did some of my best work at my summer and winter dacha hideaways. Those days set up a rhythm in my life—time with others, and time alone—that stays with me today.

Technique

Toward the end of one particularly icy winter, the snows had melted from the roadways enough to allow me to drive the forty kilometers to the church and monastery complex of Zagorsk. This site is much visited by foreign tourists: the huge blue domes painted with gold stars embody all their fantasies of old Russia. I was very lucky to be there on a beautiful sunny day, and was able to photograph the church with its snowy surroundings, the kind of scene that I love. The trees in front the church, making a pattern of branches against the stone, were very old, and drew attention to the immense age of this religious complex, built in the sixteenth century.

I wanted "Zagorsk in Winter Light" to illustrate this quality of great age, and thought the wax batik technique would be best. It would make my painting look like a cracked and worn fresco from the church itself.

I first created the painting using the gutta resist method as usual. Then I prepared my wax treatment. Here in the States, most batik artists use a combination of half paraffin and half beeswax. But in Russia, all I had available was candles, which I melted down in a saucepan on the stove. (Today we are very health-conscious, and never work with wax without wearing a respirator or being in a well-ventilated area, preferably out of doors. The heated wax particles, once breathed in, coat the lungs, and can never be removed.)

Using a very stiff, flat-ended brush, I applied a layer of wax over the whole painting. After the wax hardened, I took the painting off its frame and crumpled the whole thing by wadding it up into a ball, cracking the wax into intricate lines. I then re-stretched the painting. Then, using a different stiff brush, I worked a layer of dark pigment—a mixture of brown, blue, and black oil paint—all over the painting, forcing the pigment to seep into the cracks in the wax.

After the pigment dried, I put the painting between several layers of newspaper and ironed it with a hot iron. This had to be repeated several times to remove as much of the wax as possible. Although the process of applying and removing the wax is very time consuming, it does have an added benefit: some wax always remains in the painting and has the effect of sealing in the colors for greater permanency.

Zagorsk in Winter Light

16 The Cruise

One of my Moscow friends, Zoya, and her French husband, Roland, ran a successful importing business that involved a lot of travel between Paris, Odessa, and Moscow. As a result, Zoya had great connections with several travel agencies. Not long after my return from Holland, she was able to arrange a coveted booking for me: I would be ticketed at a travel agent's discounted fare on a cruise ship whose passengers were almost all foreigners or very rich Russians.

The *Shostakovich* would sail for seven days from Odessa, on the Black Sea, to Marseilles, where Zoya and Roland would meet me. From there, they would take me to Paris to visit with them for two weeks, after which I would rejoin the ship and cruise the eight-day return leg from Marseilles to Yalta, another port on the Black Sea.

I had never been on a cruise, and thought I would never be able to afford one. So I felt like a child who has been given permission to eat chocolate for dinner every day for a month. I packed my things with my head full of visions of Italy and Greece: beautiful beaches, colorful fishing villages, and romantic ocean sunsets from the deck of the ship.

Our first port of call after Odessa was Istanbul. While we were cruising south on the Black Sea, all the rich, well-traveled Russians gave me two pieces of advice: first, never walk around Istanbul by yourself, because it was extremely dangerous; and second, buy lots and lots of stuff in Istanbul and sell it for bundles of money in Moscow.

Since I had read all about Istanbul's architectural wonders while at the Art Institute in Moscow, I was particularly eager to see Hagia Sophia and the Blue Mosque, two of the most famous landmarks. When I tried to interest the other women in our debarkation group in a visit to these treasures, they politely agreed, but kept chattering about their shopping plans.

When we docked, I again tried to talk the women into sightseeing, but they began squealing excitedly at a cluster of interesting-looking shops. As I bought a postcard of Hagia Sophia, the Great Mosque, I noticed a small group of young men standing nearby—about five years younger than my twenty-six—and asked them for directions to the building on my postcard. Although the boys spoke only Turkish, they indicated they would serve as our guides. The shopping fanatics disappeared down an alley of leather dealers, and I waited patiently for them to finish. But after an hour, there was no sign of them, so I motioned to the young men that I was ready to take off without my friends.

The boys took me not only to the famous mosques, but also to several local neighborhood ones, half-hidden among the houses. Pantomiming instructions, they showed me how to take my shoes off before entering, and to cover my head with a scarf. They seemed to know the history of each mosque. Even though I understood no Turkish, the dramatic architecture, with its colorful tiles and richly decorated surfaces, spoke to me directly.

My gracious guides bought me some deliciously-spiced Turkish food, and treated me with great respect. They asked me to sing them Russian songs, and responded with renditions of haunting Turkish melodies. By the time we started walking slowly back to the port, stopping along the way to sing, a full moon had risen. By midnight, we had shared a rare evening, and were immutably transported beyond our differences. Meanwhile, half the Russian travelers on the ship assumed that I had been abducted or killed, and when I showed up at a ship's bar at one o'clock in the morning, they were astonished to see that I was still alive.

By the end of a second day of wandering Istanbul's streets, I had come to love its sweet, sincere, almost childlike people, and had absorbed more of the golden city's beauty. And ignoring my Russian shipmates' advice, I didn't buy a single thing.

Three weeks before I had boarded the ship, I had seen Fellini's 1984 film *And the Ship Sails On*, a mysteriously symbolic tale about art and illusion on a luxury cruise ship sailing around the Adriatic just before World War II. I was immersed in the imagery from the film, and soon after we started, I saw everything through the director's camera lens: the passengers' frequent costume changes for each shipboard activity added to the atmosphere of a movie set, and every opening of the ornate elevator doors provided a new opportunity for a grand entrance.

The cruise ship was a floating soap opera, and as I observed and listened, I became aware that under the discreet umbrella of excellent service and luxurious meals, a whole underworld of fast romantic affairs was taking place, complete with betrayals, jealousy, and instant reconciliations. And since this collection of rich foreigners and Russians were not my crowd, I could watch each amusing scene unfold as an observer of their world.

Our ship approached the port of Syracuse before dawn, and in the early morning light, the walls of the city looked like an ancient fortress, tinged with the softest hues of pink and pearly gray. As the ship drew nearer to the buildings, new details added more and more beauty.

Ivan, a fellow Muscovite on the cruise ship, suggested over breakfast that we go ashore and explore Syracuse together. We strolled aimlessly through the narrow, ancient streets, enjoying the warmth of the sun baking our skin. The usual whistles from southern Italian men dogged my steps, and although I was pleased when they shouted, "Bellissimo!" I was a little annoyed when a group of men stopped Ivan and asked him in sign language if they could have their pictures taken with me. Why didn't they just ask me? I wasn't willing to be thought of as a man's property.

Unfortunately, it was Sunday, all the shops were closed, and no one we asked knew where we could buy a bottle of wine. Then Ivan noticed two scraggly fellows sitting by a small fountain with the all-too-familiar look of Russian alcoholics. I knew some Italian, and asked where we could buy some *vino*. Happy to have us pay them any attention at all, these unlikely tour guides showed us through tiny back-street neighborhoods, describing each as proudly as if it were the Uffizi Palace in Florence.

They led us to a small, unmarked pub under a house—not much more than a whitewashed room with a few tables and chairs—a dive that no cruise ship passenger would ever find, or even consider entering. When our bleary-eyed companions found out we were Russians, they cheered and clapped us on our backs. The *Shostakovich* was docking in Syracuse for the first time, and these fellows had never spoken to "real live Russians" before. We raised our glasses each time the drunks slurred "Gorbashhev" and "pereshhtroika," proudly demonstrating their

knowledge of two Russian words.

After we bought a bottle of Chianti, the owner of the bar revealed three huge plastic buckets of home-brewed wine he had hidden under the counter—one red, one white, and one rosé—and poured us gifts, "for the friendship of our nations," into three two-liter plastic Pepsi bottles. It was actually better than the bottled wine we had purchased, so Ivan and I spent the next day at sea on the upper deck, cheerfully drunk on the unexpected bounty from our shore excursion.

Since I had overslept and missed the official cruise tour, I saw Barcelona through the windows of a taxi. But the driver knew the way to all the wonderful Antonio Gaudi architecture, with its stalagtite forms and fountains inlaid with mosaics.

When we docked at the port of Marseilles, Zoya and Roland, the Parisian friends who had arranged the cruise for me met the ship, picked me up, and headed their Mercedes toward the main highway for Paris. The sight of the city through the rear window brought back memories of my first visit, and I told them how I had wandered alone in the Old Port, oblivious to its reputation. They advised me not to do that again, but to come straight back to the ship on my return to Marseilles. There had been several news items in the papers recently about drug-related murders in the twisted, narrow alleys of the dock area.

We had a lovely visit in Paris. But I missed the rhythm of the magical days at sea. And I missed wandering freely in some of the most beautiful cities on earth—no worry about finding a place to stay or somewhere to eat—just relaxing and taking great photos, followed by an evening of comfort back on the ship.

I returned to Marseilles and the *Shostakovich* in the early morning, and ran into the ship's Russian bartender, a writer who had read some of his poems to me on the first leg of the cruise. His friend Mikhail, a Russian journalist, suggested that the three of us go together and see the sights of Marseilles, as the ship wouldn't leave until the evening.

But architecture and scenery weren't on their wish list. Mikhail wanted to videotape a porn shop, "for journalistic reasons," and the bartender wanted to buy a gun. Could I possibly help them? Neither of them spoke a word of French, and by then the bartender knew I spoke the language fluently. I had made it through Istanbul without getting sold into white slavery, so I thought this should be an interesting adventure.

At the sex shop, it was left to me to explain to the owner why the journalist wanted to videotape the store, but not purchase anything. I had never seen any of these toys before, and it was hard to keep a straight face as Mikhail earnestly filmed the assortment of devices. So far, so good. But then we entered a narrow alley with stores full of every variety of weapon—grenades, explosives, and high-tech machine guns. As we walked along in search of the perfect weapon, I noticed that there were burly hoodlums hanging out at the end of the street.

I breathed a sigh of relief as the bartender finally chose a Beretta and stowed it in his duffel bag. My Russian fatalism has given me the freedom to court danger in my search for first-hand experiences, but I won't be back to the Old Port of Marseilles anytime soon...

The weather was calm and sunny on the return leg of the cruise, and the ship's decks were the perfect place to wear my romantic, hand-painted silk garments, which moved fluidly and seductively in the soft breeze. A group of very pretty French girls from the balcony deck offered to model my clothes for me, and I shot some of the best pictures of my silk creations I've ever taken. Beautiful women, hand-painted silk, and exquisite scenery for backdrops—I was elated. But when I got back to Moscow, all but one roll of film was stolen at the developers, so I never got to see most of my photographs.

Genoa was lovely, and dirty Naples had a wild, out-of-control energy—ancient and beautiful, but very tough. I actually saw a man on a motorcycle rip a gold earring from a woman's ear as he sped by.

Athens was our last port of call. The Acropolis was a precious jewel, and I knew every stone of it by heart from my architecture studies. Brilliant white walls in full sun and a stunning turquoise sea presented a challenge to a painter on silk; there was no softness—none of the subtlety of the Italian light.

Often, at night, I went to the uppermost deck of the cruise ship and lay down with my feet in the narrow tip of the vessel. As I felt the movement of the ship underneath me, and listened to music on my tape player, I would look at the sky, full of thousands of stars—an ever-changing design that moved slowly over me. These were precious moments, full of an expansive beauty. Several of my best paintings came into my mind's eye during those hours I spent dreaming under the stars.

I imagined a woman lying nude on the window seat in Dima's studio. The garden of the Pushkin Museum would drift behind her, dreamlike, as she lay complete within herself: the lover and the beloved. Although it had been eight years since this first love, I still strongly felt the emotions attached to that time of my life. I planned to paint this picture as soon as I returned to Moscow.

Technique

By the time we had reached Genoa, I had fallen in love with Italy, and it has become, far and above, my favorite place to paint. "Misty Facade, Genoa" was one of many paintings I did of Genovese buildings and street scenes.

Even a painting like this one, which has the effortlessness and immediacy of a sketch, has been carefully composed in advance. Although I don't expect my students to spend months preparing the sketches for a painting like the grand masters did, composition is a very important tool in the creation of any painting, no matter how simple or complex.

I am happy with this painting because it incorporates almost all of the elements I love to depict: buildings, reflections in windows, and figures. I kept the composition from being too busy by using large areas of un-detailed dark color to simplify certain elements, such as the prominent columns in the foreground and the interiors of the three archways. The only spots of really warm color are on the figures of the two girls, which bring them forward in the space and allow everything else to recede. The reflections in the windows, although very complex, have balanced shapes in mirror images, giving the viewer a sense of rest, even though there is a lot going on in the painting. There is just the tiniest bit of salt in the central window, where there might be a temptation to overdo it. The reflections are painted in muted tones with just a little less definition than the stones of the first floor archways, and this also helps them to recede upwards.

I painted the topmost balcony and windows in the palest of blue-grays, and kept detail to a minimum, giving a hint of the seaport city's misty, salty, ocean air. And the figures of the girls remind me achingly of the beauty of the stolen photographs of my hand-painted silk clothing that I took during the cruise— images that I'll never be able to see.

Misty Facade, Genoa

и не в верхней [illegible]

[illegible] или ничего не интересно

или фантазия, (может быть я и не права)

Но мне сейчас очень интересно

[illegible] жить, самое всего, [illegible]

нет а может она и не нужна?

[illegible]. Вчера было что то страшное [illegible]

[illegible] перед тем как [illegible]

[illegible]

[illegible] Теперь я смотрю что то [illegible]

[illegible]

[illegible] девочками. [illegible] интересно

[illegible]

[illegible] всё время. [illegible]

[illegible]

[illegible] Вчера я [illegible] страшные вещи

[illegible]

[illegible] для того чтобы [illegible]

[illegible] а [illegible] себе, что я [illegible]

17 Moscow

Three days after my return from the cruise, I ran into Dima again. It was a sultry mid-July day, just before my twenty-seventh birthday, and I had been walking along the Boulevard Ring, central Moscow's circular roadway, with its two directions of bustling traffic divided by a narrow but pleasant park. There he was, sitting on a bench, smoking and reading a small volume of poetry. He looked up as if he had been expecting me—as if we had just parted a week ago—then invited me up to his studio for tea. As we rode the Metro, I glanced at him several times, noticing streaks of gray in his dark hair. He seemed tired, worn down by life. But I felt our long-dormant physical and spiritual connection drawing me to him again—a trance of attraction. Behind the door of his studio once more, I moved first into his arms, and then into his bed. It had been eight years since we lay together like this.

After making love, I reminisced about our chance meeting. The park bench where I had found him was miles from my favorite old haunts: the charming, narrow streets near his studio overlooking the garden of the Pushkin Museum. Was it just a coincidence that our paths had intersected? Or had the vision of me lying on his window seat, so powerfully formed in my mind's eye that starry night on the prow of the cruise ship, led me back to him? We Russians are great believers in fate, and for some inexplicable reason here I was, in Dima's embrace again.

He rose from the bed and moved over to the tall open window, making a soft trilling call with his tongue. In flew a lustrous black raven flapping white-banded wings that Dima had named Karlusha. While she ate scraps of chicken that he scattered on the windowsill, he explained that the great bird lived in the garden of the Pushkin, but often came to eat these tidbits and to chuckle and cluck from a perch on the iron bed frame. At once, I knew that Karlusha needed to be in a painting I had envisioned on the cruise. The raven would represent my soul, freely soaring above my body as it did in "Flight," traveling the cosmic distances that cannot be measured in miles.

I saw Dima two or three times a month, but I was a different woman, and flew in and out of his life like Karlusha—a part of him, but not fully belonging to him as before. I had my artistic life, my paintings and ceramics, and my friends, and he soon sensed that I would never again be the adoring teenager who once held him in awe. He hated my having a master stronger than he was: my dedication to my work. And he was jealous of my experiences in foreign places he had never seen, and my knowledge of the world outside Soviet borders. He became angry when I left him to paint, and accused me of growing distant. Though we continued to sleep together for over a year—our physical connection still as strong as ever—our relationship inevitably began to collapse under the weight of the same arguments and mind games that had caused me to leave him the first time.

I turned to my circle of friends to help me get over Dima once and for all. The hub of my social life was a group of six girlfriends who would meet to sit in the sauna at the huge Sandunovskie Baths, Moscow's most famous public bathhouse, or *banya*. It was right across from my studio, fortuitously located in the center of the city, near the Bolshoi Theater.

In northern countries like Finland and Russia, the banya has little to do with washing: it's a place for meeting your friends and talking. My first encounter with the sauna had been during a cross-country ski trip to Karelia, formerly an autonomous Soviet republic just to the east of Finland. Seven of us from the city took a two-week-long excursion, skiing many miles a day and sleeping in rustic log guest houses in the birch woods. At the end of trips such as these, it was a tradition for the group to have a sauna together, run outside, and plunge into icy water through a hole cut in a frozen lake. Ever since then, I have always loved the sauna and have never missed an opportunity to take one.

At the Sandunovskie, we enjoyed our sauna in an atmosphere of faded elegance. In the nineteenth century, the huge marble swimming pool had been surrounded by sculptures, and priceless oil paintings hung on the walls. The gilded wooden carvings were now chipped and layered with dust, and the crystal chandeliers were missing half their ornaments. But the steam and sauna were the best in town, and my five girlfriends and I never missed our weekly sessions there. We brought tea and fruit to share; gave each other massages; put masques of honey and salt on our faces; and covered our hair with woolen ski caps to keep it from being damaged by the sauna's heat. After hours together, baking away our cares and unburdening our hearts, we'd come out into the freezing air of a sub-zero winter's night, feeling renewed and reborn.

I knew it was time to get a divorce from Etienne and free myself up for a chance at a good marriage. Although I had been dreading another round of endless paperwork and standing in lines, the process was easier than I had imagined: Soviet officialdom appreciated the propaganda value of a daughter of the Soviet Union choosing to come back and stay in Russia after living in France. So only one set of papers and two visits to the central Moscow bureau finalized the divorce.

I sent the divorce papers to Etienne, expecting the usual round of angry phone calls in response. To my surprise, he did not call me. Perhaps he had finally realized I was never going to come back to him. At least there was a reprieve in his attempts to deny that it was over between us.

One Monday, I dropped by the art studio on Petrovka Street where I was still teaching a group of students. It was a disaster: someone had evidently bribed the local housing official, who had given my space to the person who greased his palm. All my books and art materials had disappeared, as well as the hundreds of things I'd collected for still life painting, like bottles, shells, and fabrics. Over the weekend, everything had been dumped into the courtyard behind the building—treated like trash. I salvaged what I could, and having no place to keep my supplies, gave most of them away to friends. I still feel sad when I think of the loss of that wonderful art space.

Luckily, my neighbor Sasha and my sauna girlfriends provided comic relief from Dima's gloomy tirades and the loss of my studio. For a while, I owned both the blue Volvo and a beat-up Lada. One or the other was always breaking down, so my friend Misha called the cramped courtyard outside babushka's apartment "Natasha's Museum of Broken Cars."

Sasha would hail me cheerfully in the courtyard as I attempted to race off to a friend's studio—stuffing some paintings into the back of whichever car was running—and would suggest repairs for the broken-down one by launching into a detailed description of exactly what he had done to fix his own carburetor or radiator or windshield wiper. I had to conceal my impatience with his unbelievably long explanations: it was probably the only chance the poor guy—a few strands of blond hair plastered in strings across his shiny, pink head—ever had to talk to a woman, and he was going to make the most of it.

Sasha was ridiculously proud of his own nondescript car, a Lada he had trussed up with a jury-rigged system of consecutive locking devices that he claimed no burglar could ever defeat. One day I found his car blocking mine inside our gated courtyard, and my friend Anna's boyfriend, Ilya, needed my car to get to a job interview. Sasha was nowhere to be found, and I told Ilya it was impossible to thwart Sasha's anti-burglar defense system. But Ilya just snorted with derision, broke into the car in about two seconds, and pushed it past the courtyard gates so he could drive mine out into the street.

When Sasha returned from work, he stood staring at his car parked in the street as if his whole universe had collapsed. His thin, bluish lips moved up and down, but no sound came out. I felt so sorry for him that I made up a ridiculous story about "really having to get my car out so we had hired a crane to lift his car out of the courtyard. . ." I just couldn't admit that we had broken through his three-ruble locks. He would never have forgiven me.

That September, my Volvo was running well, so I was still painting at my summer dacha in Troitskoe. Ordinarily, the weather didn't turn very cold until October, but my attic room, with its beautiful view of meadows and trees, had no heater, and an arctic wind had blown down from the Gulf of Finland. Dressed in a warm coat and fingerless gloves to protect my hands, I was working on a painting I call "Mediterranean Still Life."

A table floated in the foreground, its top decorated with a few of my favorite objects: a ceramic Japonaise vase made by Marita in Riga, a fancifully-shaped tropical seashell, and a wine bottle from my recent cruise. I had bought this particular bottle of wine in Naples, and had spent the next day at sea, drinking with cruise buddies on the deck and enjoying our view of the Sicilian coastline. In one of my photographs from the trip, the bottle glowed in the reflected golden light of the setting sun. So in the painting, I worked on creating the feeling of the open expanse of the sea and the peachy-gold sky.

I hung the painting on the wall to see how well I had created the effect of the Mediterranean sunset. As I watched, I began to feel warmth coming out of the painting—an actual, palpable glow which radiated out from the stretched silk on the wall. Just then, my friend Misha walked in. He had been going to a sanitorium nearby for a recurring numbness in his legs, and often bicycled over to chat and see what I was working on. He, too, could feel the warmth coming out of the painting.

It wasn't the first time strange things had occured with my paintings. When I returned from my stay in the hospital for liver failure, one of the paintings in my apartment had fallen to the floor, and another hung so crookedly it was almost upside down. No one had been in the apartment while I was away, but Misha says that your energy field changes when you are ill, and that some part of your energy resides in your paintings in some mysterious form.

The cold arctic blast of that September of 1989 wasn't the only unusual wind blowing into my world. Even with the loss of my Moscow studio, I was happily immersed in my life as an artist, surrounded by good friends, and selling enough paintings to keep myself going. But my ordinary, contented existence would soon change forever: that was the year I met Sarah.

Technique

"Dreamscape" was my first attempt to paint a nude woman on silk. I now overlook the technical mistakes—of which there are many—because it is my favorite piece, one that I will never part with. It's hanging over my bed now: I brought it back from Russia in a suitcase. I find it difficult to write about this painting objectively, since it is full of the emotions from that very special time in my life with Dima. Like my friend Misha, I feel that the most personal paintings hold a resonance of the energy field of the painter. In any case, this painting gets crooked frequently.

I have always loved drawing nudes. For years in Moscow, I went to a life drawing class every Sunday and sketched the models for several hours. The problem with painting a nude on silk is that any resist lines in the interior of the figure make it look like a cartoon character. But a whole body is much bigger than a face, and it must be executed in a very short period of time, before the silk dries. Currently I am challenging myself to do a series of full-sized nude figures, and I have been able to paint a figure as big as the one in "Dreamscape," including a face, in a half hour.

In this piece, I first painted the background color of the figure. But a flesh tone just wouldn't work, as I wanted to depict a very early morning scene in that flat, grayish light before sunrise. I had to know human anatomy in order to be able to put the shadows in the right places: the shadows outlining the muscles and shapes of bones must have rounded edges, and highlighting some areas with reflected light from the white sheets helped to make the shapes round. Very carefully, I painted the colors of the shadows, rubbing them in with an almost dry brush so they would lie perfectly.

For the rest of the painting, I used the tilt of the open windows and buildings and a watery, washy, salt-splashed style to give the feeling of an imaginary dreamscape. Karlusha, the raven, is rendered in the same grays as the nude, making him part of me and not a piece of background imagery.

Dreamscape

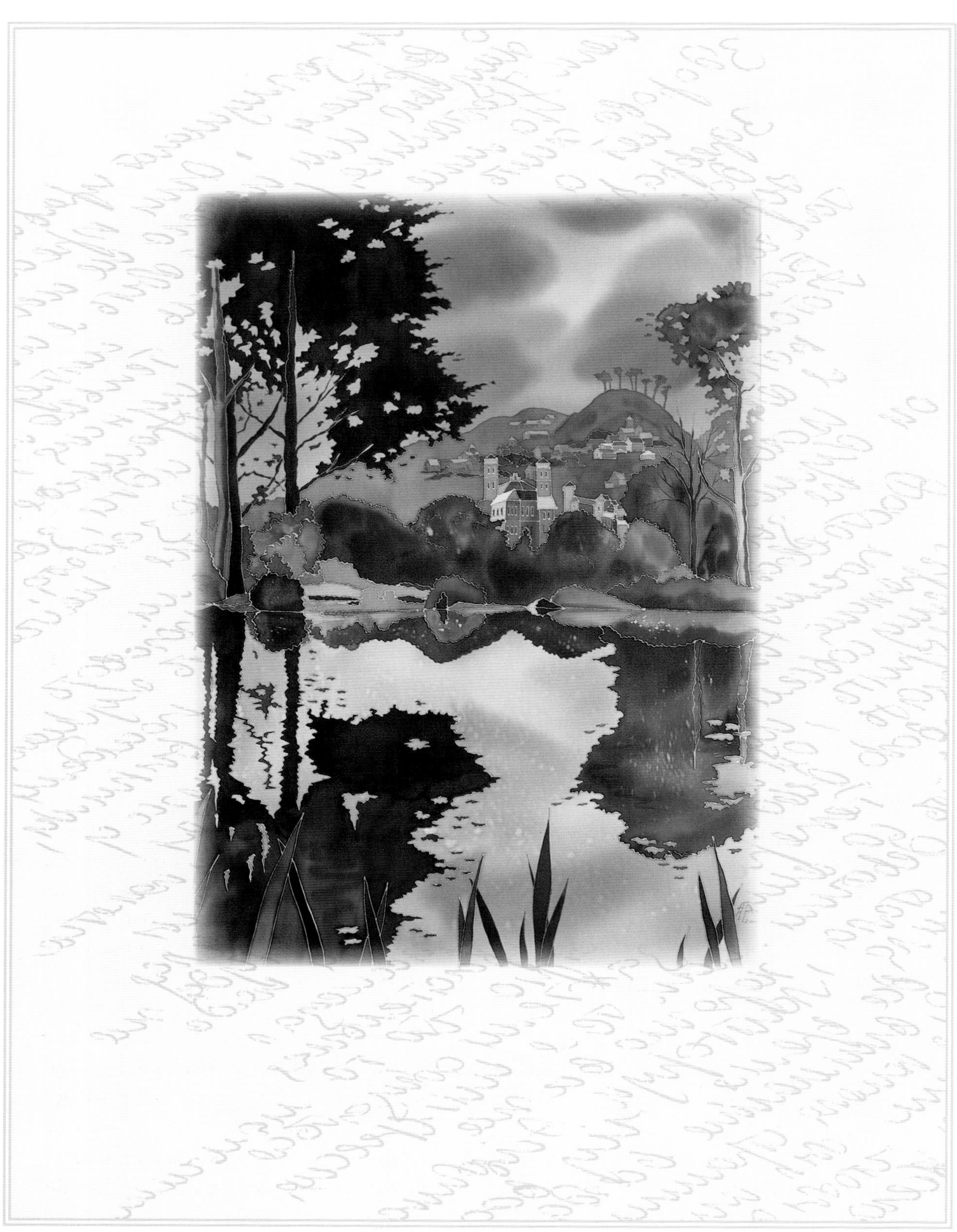

18 San Francisco

With her Australian sheepherder's coat, torn blue jeans, and purple alligator cowboy boots, Sarah turned heads everywhere she went in Moscow. This multi-talented powerhouse of a woman had come to Russia to visit a girlfriend who was teaching in a Berkeley exchange program, and had fallen in love with the country. If Sarah focused the lighthouse beam of her huge talents and unflagging energy on a project, she succeeded at it. By turns a biologist, city councilwoman, computer whiz, truck driver, and business startup guru, she had decided, with encouragement from my art dealer friend, Sergei, to cash in on the hotness of Russian art that began in the early Gorbachev days.

Sharing a ravenous appetite for adventure, Sarah and I became the best of friends. Her business card read, "Director, Russian Art and Cultural Center, San Francisco Bay Area"—a lofty title that I couldn't quite reconcile with her cowboy boots and infectious laughter. But then I had never been to California. . .

Sarah spent the New Year holidays at my dacha in Peredelkino during the winter of 1990. Then, when no sane person would have traveled, and just for the sheer impossibility of it, we took a trip across the Black Sea to Odessa in a decrepit little passenger boat full of drunk students and Georgians. As we shivered in our cabin, which was lit by a single flickering light bulb, Sarah urged me to come to California and have a show of my paintings in her gallery, where she had been collecting and displaying Russian art.

But I had absolutely no desire to visit the United States. Like any other Soviet young person, I had been raised on a steady diet of negative media images of our Cold War enemy—rats in the subways, inner-city poverty, people queued up outside soup kitchens that we couldn't know had been closed since the Depression. And my travels in Europe had exposed me to the widely-held opinion that America was a country of uneducated dolts. Everyone made private jokes about the American tourists in Paris and Venice, with their unfashionable Nike sneakers and cameras dangling around their sunburned necks. So even though Sarah's energy and enthusiasm kept me intrigued about California, I waited several months before I decided to apply for a visa.

My opinions about America weren't the only drawback: it took three weeks to get to the front of the visa application line at the American Embassy, so people with jobs would hire an unemployed friend or an older relative to stand in the line for them. But several months later, in the summer of 1990, Sergei phoned and said that if I still wanted to go to the States, he had a place close to the front of the line. With so many people standing in for each other, no one would notice if I turned up in front of him.

I was sure that I would be rejected. I would have to prove that I wouldn't just jump ship and stay in America—that I was married, or had a good job, or owned some property—anything that would ensure my return to Russia. But of course, I had none of these things.

Finally, I decided to queue up at the Embassy, just so Sergei wouldn't think I was chicken-hearted. When I got to the front of the line, I saw three windows: the one on the left was occupied. There was no line before the middle window, but the grim official had KGB written all over his mask-like face. And a garrulous woman was holding things up on the right. Something made me decide to wait for the far right window, even if it meant I would wait longer.

At the window, a very young woman began peppering me with the usual questions: "What reason do we have to believe you won't stay in the United States?"

"Are you kidding?" I laughed. "I was married to a Frenchman in France, and I left him to come back here and live in Moscow. I like my life here. I don't have the slightest desire to stay in America."

I explained my invitation to have an exhibit of my paintings on silk in California. The girl's eyes lit up with excitement: she loved silk painting and wanted to come to my studio and see my work. Inexplicably, she handed me the thin yellow visa. I was utterly astonished.

Later, when the young embassy worker and I met for tea at my studio, she bought a painting from me, and I learned why she had given me a visa: she was a student at the Pushkin Language Institute, just a temporary replacement for one of the nasty regulars who had been strictly trained to reject people like me.

By the end of the summer, I still hadn't made up my mind to use the visa. Soon it would be autumn, my favorite time of year, and I was looking forward to the orange, red and yellow of the frost-nipped trees. It was a very prolific and creative period in my artistic life: I was completing a painting a day, working from my cruise photographs and inspired by the beauty of Italy. Reunited with the love of my life, I still had plenty of time for the solitude I needed for painting, and lots of friends to do things with when I wanted to cut loose. The visa to the States had been handed to me by accident, and I was reluctant to go. Why should I?

My friends and I couldn't yet see the significance of Gorbachev's reforms, his *perestroika* and *glastnost*. Although Gorby's leadership was receiving recognition abroad, the Russian economy was badly stagnating, and there were serious food and fuel shortages: sugar and vodka had become our main currency. We even had rationing cards, making chicken a luxury. But I wasn't seeing the bigger picture, cocooned as I was in my artistic world of painting, friends, and Dima.

My mother, however, urged me to go to America and just check it out before it was "too

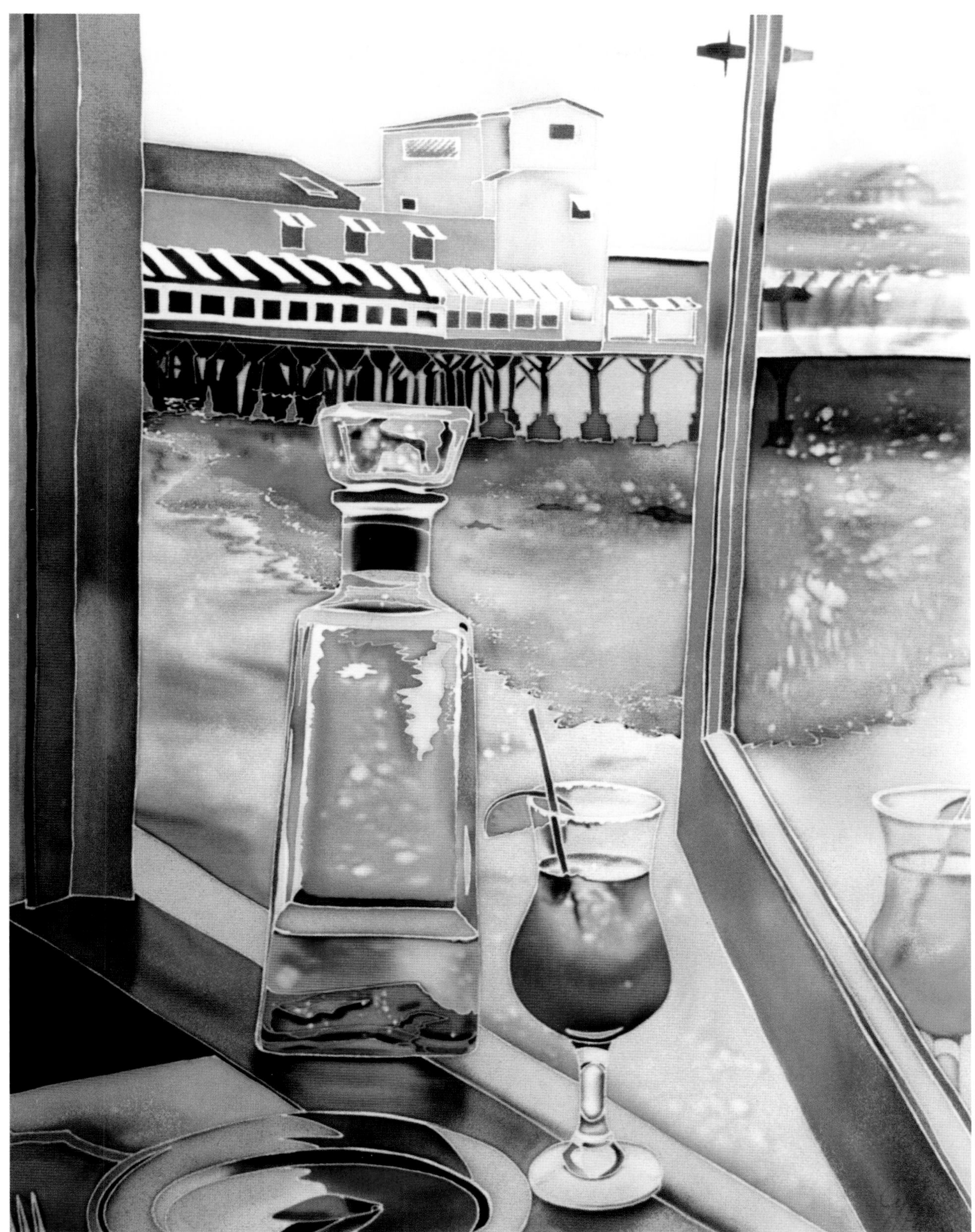

Cannery Row, Monterey

late." Her job as a chemist working in a lab full of politically savvy citizens kept her much more well-informed than I was. With hindsight, it seems to the world now that the reforms were a steady path toward capitalism and a more Western-style democracy. But at the time, wiser, experienced adults like my mother knew that things could just as easily go wrong—very, very, wrong—and there could be a brutal crackdown the likes of which we hadn't seen since Stalin.

Still ambivalent about the journey, I finally bought my plane ticket. And at my summer dacha, I wrote the last entry from Russia in my diary, two days before the flight that took me to New York: "I have a sense of great anticipation. Something momentous is about to happen, I may never be able to resume my old life. Yet I am already missing Russia..."

There were no direct flights to San Francisco, so I flew into New York. An old girlfriend, now married to the same Genna who had visited me in the hospital while pretending to be a doctor, had immigrated to America with him, and the couple greeted me with dozens of hugs at Kennedy Airport. Staying with them for four days, I found New York to be an amazing place. But during many visits since then, I've felt the city's enormously oppressive power: all the high rise buildings make me feel like an ant, and I am always glad to leave.

After hours of staring up at the skyscrapers of Manhattan, my only respite was strolling through the green open spaces of Central Park. It was early fall, and I was delighted by the reflections of the high rises in the park's lakes and by the brilliant autumn colors, which inspired several paintings later on.

I arrived at San Francisco International Airport and was embraced by my friend Sarah, who took me straight to the Cliff House on San Francisco's westernmost edge. It was the quintessential place to experience the beauty of the city and its spirit.

When the "Russian Cultural Center" turned out to be Sarah's garage in Vallejo, a suburb across the bay from the luminous San Francisco, I was quite shocked. I had been expecting at least two or three buildings, with marble columns and stairways, a wing of art studios, and locker rooms for art supplies. But with a real Russian living there among the stacks of paintings and folk art, perhaps the garage had finally earned its lofty name!

I had a lovely stay with Sarah and her warm and friendly family, but Vallejo lived up to all my images of America's ugliness. I was visually bludgeoned by the wasteland of gas stations, strip malls, identical housing tracts, and freeways cutting up the landscape wherever I looked. Although I decided to stay for the full six months of my visa, and Sarah organized a successful show of my paintings, I was definitely looking forward to going back home.

However, a Russian friend I met in San Francisco had been traveling on a remarkably inexpensive ticket sold to foreigners. Flying standby on Delta, one could go anywhere in the States for a whole month, and I couldn't pass up this incredible deal.

Traveling that way was uncomplicated: airplanes simply became my home, and I felt as free as a bird. It was February of 1991, during the Gulf War—fewer Americans were travelling—and I could get a seat on almost any flight, taking in the United States from coast to coast—twenty-two cities in all.

My network of Russians in America grew as each visit to a new city added names to the list of people with whom I could stay. In Santa Fe, with its unique adobe architecture and vibrant art community, I connected with a woman photographer who introduced me to the little church in nearby Chimayo, famous for its healing powers. Tropical Miami bathed my spirit in its warm glow, and I overcame my fear of sharks so I could take a long swim in the Atlantic Ocean. I skied in New England and skated at Rockefeller Center, then spent a whole day in the National Gallery in Washington, D.C. New Orleans touched me deeply as the center of American jazz life, with its crumbling French Quarter and Southern style.

These new impressions of the United States totally replaced those Soviet images of Depression-era soup kitchens from the black and white newsreels. And now, having visited most of the major cities on the continent, I returned to San Francisco, and appreciated even more its temperate climate, Victorian architecture stacked on steep hillsides, and sparkling ocean views. My eyes were opening to new possibilities, but my future was still uncertain.

Technique

"Cliff House" is painted from a photo taken that first day with Sarah. It's a happy painting, and although I did it much later, the feeling of my first hours in San Francisco is very much evident. I loved the view, and returning many times after that, I made Cliff House my touchstone for everything that was bright and vibrant in San Francisco.

My friends have quietly resigned themselves to the fact that I must take pictures of the glasses before they can enjoy drinks or a meal in a restaurant. And my first visit was no exception.

What attracted me most on this occasion was the effect of the foam dripping down the sides of the beer glasses. To capture the intricate shapes it made, I needed to have an excellent photograph, because shapes dreamed up from the imagination tend to look false. Sometimes I must add resist lines because of the need in silk painting to have enclosed spaces, but I must be very careful with these.

For the amber beer, I didn't want any white resist lines. As always, I first enclosed all the white areas in the painting with resist, including the all-important foam. Then I painted the beer areas yellow, built up the reflections in the beer glasses with successive layers of resist outlines and darker colors, and softened the reflections of the cliffs inside the glasses with salt to make them less solid. Finally, I treated the ocean and sky with a very watery wash and plenty of salt to keep the focus of the painting on the table.

This painting clearly shows how my palette changed when I came to America. Its colors are outrageously bright compared to my earlier work: pure turquoise, strong amber tones for the beer, the reds and oranges in the nachos. In Russia, I had read that the colors of your surroundings gradually penetrate your psyche, and it must be true, because the bright colors I so disliked at home began to appear more and more frequently as time went on.

When I must paint with my former palette of muted colors and pastels, I find it to be quite difficult. For instance, when I'm working on commission on a very gray, monochromatic scene of St. Petersburg, sitting in my brightly-lit California studio with a brilliant blue sky outside, I must consciously focus on the photographs at hand, and remind myself to mute the colors with every brushful of dye. Even with that extra effort, I am still losing my touch for my earlier palette, and must accept my gradual evolution into a California painter with strong Russian roots.

Cliff House

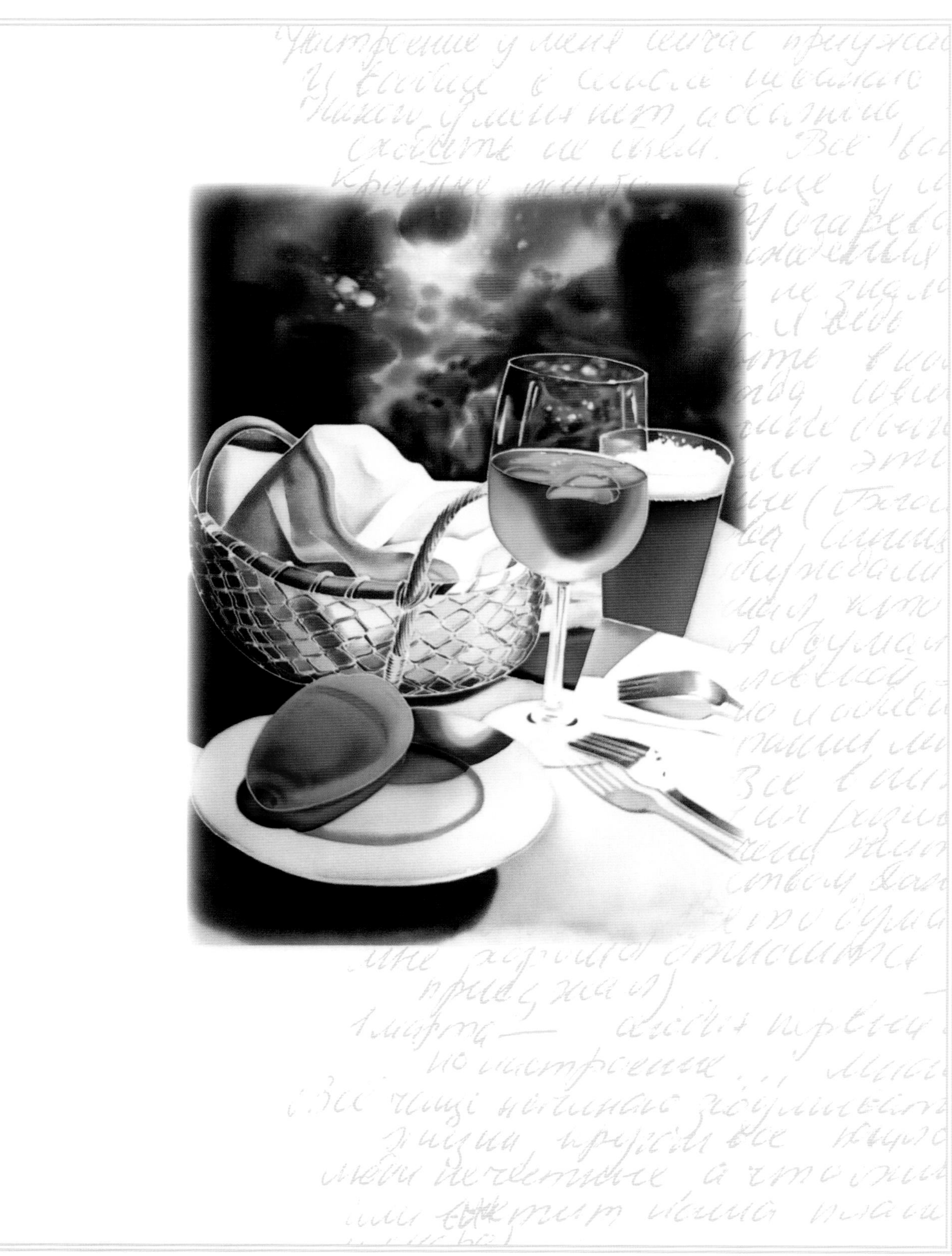

19 Safe Harbor

From my temporary home in Sarah's Vallejo garage, I started to give silk painting classes. At first, my only students were Sarah's neighbors, but soon the circle expanded and I was quite busy. One neighbor's daughter and her boyfriend offered to take me camping in Yosemite; and a few weekends later, we were snuggled into a beige Winnebago cruising through an extraordinarily beautiful valley, dwarfed by the towering rock walls that make this park so spectacular.

One late afternoon, after climbing up to Nevada Falls by myself, I didn't leave enough time to get back to the campsite before dark. I remembered that the camper was parked next to a bridge, but after I passed several identical bridges and wandered by hundreds of campsites in the dark, all the vehicles and tents began to look the same. Almost in a panic, I stumbled up to our campsite two hours later. And before I had a chance to untie my boots, a park ranger knocked on our door and asked for Natasha. Someone named Sarah had called and wanted to talk to me as soon as possible.

I was frightened for an instant, then relieved. In the split second after the ranger had spoken my name, I thought that the KGB had hunted me down. Who else could find me hundreds of miles from the nearest city? In Russia, once my family was off camping in the middle of a forest, we were out of touch completely: we would simply drive up to a secluded spot almost anywhere, pull out our gear by the side of the road, and start boiling water for tea. So when I learned about the computerized registration system that Sarah had used to find us, it seemed a bit silly to herd all the campers into side-by-side, numbered campsites like cows in their stalls. But for the moment, I gratefully followed the ranger back to the telephone at park headquarters.

"Natasha, we have to be in Weaverville tomorrow. There's going to be a big Russian art festival with a theater group from Russia performing. It's going to be a huge event and they want to have as many Russian artists exhibiting as possible. . ."

Sarah's excitement was like a forest fire, sweeping me up in its path. I had no idea where Weaverville was, but found myself negotiating California's freeway system for the first time the next morning at the wheel of a small second car my friends had driven to Yosemite.

I was an experienced driver in Russia (if not the most skilled), but the little piece of paper on which Jim scribbled a series of highway numbers and exits did not show the tangle of complicated lane changes, and I zigzagged wildly across four lanes of traffic several times, narrowly avoiding catastrophe. That same night, Sarah and I piled into her jeep and picked up a Russian architect friend, Vadim. He was visiting San Francisco, and wanted to see what a Russian art festival in the wilds of northern California would be like.

After driving all night, we were delighted by the glow of the sunrise on the volcanic peak of Mount Shasta. It was Thanksgiving time, and each turn of the road—a Grand Prix challenge on the breathtakingly narrow, twisting highway heading west out of Redding—revealed vistas splashed with the last of the autumn color and scattered patches of early snow. We arrived at the tiny mountain artists' community of Weaverville, and Sarah and Vadim helped to set up my paintings.

Later that evening, in a cowboy bar, the performers from the Russian theater group overheard our conversation, and asked Vadim where he had learned his Russian. "At Stanford, of course!" he joked.

When the actors discovered that Vadim and I were from Moscow, as were they, our new friends were amazed to have found educated Russians in this mountain hideaway. And they were more than a little embarrassed—afraid that the simple pieces they had performed that evening might not be up to our highbrow Moscow standards.

Of the several really lovely people we met at my art show, one was a woman named Candace, who bought two of my paintings: the first, a Leningrad scene; and another, a still life of wine glasses on a table in Amsterdam. Her daughter, Karen, was studying Russian, and was preparing to leave for Moscow. And Candace, a midwife who had traveled all over the world, was eager to talk some more about Russia after my show, so she invited us to stay that night at her farm outside Weaverville.

"Here's a map showing how to get there. Just come when you're ready, we'll be waiting for you," Karen's mother smiled warmly. How could I warn this friendly woman that it could be dawn before a bunch of drunk Russians talking over their Moscow experiences might be ready to call it a day?

But we were in no condition to return to the Bay Area that night, and attempted the drive to Candace's farm. After an hour of wrong turns, dead ends, and crazy meanderings up ridges and down into seemingly bottomless, dark valleys, we saw the welcome beacon of glowing lights from the farmhouse. And to our amazement, Candace and her husband, Arnold, were waiting up for us after midnight.

The next morning, we found ourselves in a gorgeous wooden house on a hilltop—the fields below us blanketed in fog, and craggy mountain peaks creating a spectacular view in every direction. (My painting "Sunny Afternoon" shows the house, with its wooden screen door and rocking chair on the wrap-around porch.) We left the next morning, knowing that Candace's invitation for us to return was genuine, and that I would come back again.

Before she left for Moscow, Karen invited me to meet her in the wine-country town of Sonoma to participate in Orthodox Christmas festivities with her Serbian-American family. Both Russians and Serbians celebrate Christmas Eve on January 6th, Epiphany, the night the three kings found the baby Jesus lying in his stable in Bethlehem.

I was delighted to see that such a large group of people, all born in America, still kept alive their traditions, such as lavish spreads of Serbian food: stuffed cabbage, kasha, chicken broth with dumplings, breads with coins baked inside—and of course, brightly decorated cookies. There were baptisms by an Orthodox priest for the year's crop of babies, and Serbian dancing. I felt warmly encircled by the comfort of shared traditions and remembrances of my own family's holidays. And Michael, one of Candace's cousins, invited me to his church in San Francisco the following week for more dancing, in celebration of Serbian New Year.

The festivities went on until the wee hours of a stormy morning, and Michael suggested that I spend the night with one of his relatives living in the city, rather than risk a drive over the Bay Bridge to Vallejo in the wind and rain. So we drove through the narrow, winding streets in a dense fog—so thick and impenetrable that I couldn't tell where we were going. As we got out of the car, Michael explained that we were in a little hillside neighborhood clinging to the base of Twin Peaks in the southeastern part of San Francisco.

He knocked on an unpainted wooden door that looked so much like a Russian dacha entryway that I thought I was dreaming. When a dark-haired man opened the door, I recognized him as Steve, a cousin of Michael's I had briefly met at the church.

As I took off my coat in the high-ceilinged hallway and walked into the main room, I fell instantaneously in love with the house. It had worn wooden floors, dark and heavily-carved

furniture, and a tall antique mirror in the dining room. I felt the calm of the house wrap around me like a blanket as I looked out a huge window, where fog-shrouded trees were ghostly silhouettes in the narrow, steep back yard. The house was unbelievably clean and peaceful, and I remember thinking, *a woman must live here*. . . But when I opened the refrigerator and found it empty except for a quart of milk, I knew I was mistaken. . .

The next morning, I went to look for Steve and Michael, but couldn't find them. At last, I located a narrow stairway to a separate wing of living quarters that had been constructed on the hillside under the older main house. Like many San Francisco dwellings, this one took advantage of every buildable square foot.

Michael and Steve were quietly talking, and Steve had a little parakeet sitting on his shoulder, which he was including in the conversation as if she were another person. A strong feeling of tenderness and recognition flowed though me—warm like a flow of hot water from a source inside my belly. In that instant, my life changed its course.

Steve and I began seeing each other, although it wasn't a very likely courtship. Starting a relationship was the furthest thing from my mind. I would soon be returning to Russia, I thought, and my artist's life. Steve had been in several relationships and two marriages, and had decided that bachelorhood, although sometimes lonely, would be his choice for the rest of his life.

Quiet and unassuming, Steve was nothing like the much more gregarious and flamboyant men I had been involved with before. An electrician who was several years older than I was, he found San Francisco, where he had been born and raised, a most satisfying place, and had little desire to live anywhere else. Both of us were surprised at the speed with which we found ourselves wanting to be together all the time. I moved into his house in February, and we began taking weekend trips to the Big Sur coast, the wine country, and Mendocino.

It didn't make any sense to me that I was falling in love, but I was. Steve surprised himself too, as his fear of getting hurt again began to be replaced by trust. I'd had an uncanny sense of homecoming when I first saw that little bird on his shoulder, and the tenderness he showed his avian companion melted my heart. And of all the cities I had visited in the States, San Francisco had the strongest Russian immigrant community, so I felt at home in the foggy city overlooking the bay. But my visa was about to expire.

"I suppose I should go back to Russia," I sighed one day.

"I suppose you shouldn't," replied Steve.

This may have been the most low-key marriage proposal ever made in recorded history, but it sounded sweeter to me than a dozen more romantic offers.

Both of us had suffered through previous marriage ceremonies featuring embarrassingly huge white bridal gowns, and neither of us wanted to make a big splash in front of a crowd of family and friends. So we went quietly off to Fairfield near the San Francisco Bay Delta, where we had a small civil ceremony, and honeymooned on Steve's boat.

Actually, we weren't at all sure that our marriage would work. Both of us were old and wise enough to realize that our romantic connection was going to be challenged by the mundane business of daily life, our very different personalities, and the issue of my poor English and his nonexistent Russian. Then, too, there was my strong determination to remain a full-time working artist. So only time would tell.

Technique

Later, after we were married, I painted "The Wedding Bouquet" from several photographs taken on our wedding day. The bird on my hat is a reminder of the first time I saw Steve with his little parakeet.

The painting depicts a floral arrangement that was a wedding gift, in which each of the twenty types of flowers symbolized a different thing: prosperity, love, children, or happiness. I particularly liked the way the different stems inside the vase looked in the somewhat fogged glass.

First, I outlined the vase and its three square white highlights with gutta resist, along with the outlines of the stems. But to enhance the effect of the milky glass of the vase, I allowed the colors inside the stems to flow outside the resist lines by wetting the whole area inside the vase, except for the highlights, before painting it. After the colors had flowed into the vase to my satisfaction, I added a little salt.

I rarely paint flowers, because they are complete in their own beauty: a rose is perfect in nature, and I don't feel I can add anything to that perfection. And again, I always prefer to find beauty where it is unexpected; but these flowers were a remembrance of our special day.

To paint a large bouquet of flowers successfully, you must eliminate most of the leaves and blooms and include only the most striking or important ones. Try to create a focus, as I did with the two main white flowers, which create a balanced composition with the two figures. All the flowers and leaves are done with the wet-on-wet technique, and I added shape to some of the flower petals and leaves with darker tones. I used only the tiniest amount of dye for a soft, diffused, blending—blue-gray and pink and yellow, for the white flowers—and created the stamens with a line of gutta resist. The baby's breath in the background was created by making little dots of resist, and the flowers take their shape from the darker tones of the background behind them. The background is a very soft array of colors mixed with a lot of water and salt.

The faces are created, as described in earlier technique sections, with very little resist, and by controlling the dampness of the silk.

Steve hated seeing himself painted and asked me never to paint him again, and it usually wasn't hard for me to comply. (I have always preferred to paint women, as they seem to be compatible with the softness, romance, and femininity of the silk.) And the parakeet took an intense dislike to me—I guess she wanted to be the only woman in Steve's life—and bit me on the head whenever she could! Sadly, we had to give her away.

The Wedding Bouquet

Sunny Afternoon

20 Weaverville

Now that Steve and I were married, Candace and Arnold in Weaverville had become my family too, and we visited them as often as possible. During one of our first return trips to their farm, Candace had introduced us to her friends Bella and Philo. Bella had graduated from art college in England and had married the Filipino actor and carpenter in San Francisco.

Years earlier, one of Philo's army buddies tried to pay off a gambling debt by selling an enormous hunk of land "in the middle of some godforsaken mountain range in northern California." Philo bought the land, sight unseen, for a thousand dollars, and didn't even think about it for several years.

But when urban construction jobs became scarce and Bella's income as an artist couldn't pay the rent, they packed up their two-month-old baby, Palacia, and everything they owned, and moved to their land, which they discovered was on a four-thousand-foot ridge outside Weaverville. They fell in love with the mountains, put up a little shack to live in, and found a way to generate electrical power from their creek. And over the next twenty-five years, they built their dream house, one two-by-four at a time, from Philo's earnings as a construction worker.

When I first entered Bella and Philo's home with Candace, I saw a photograph of Palacia as a baby, smiling and sitting in the big clawfoot bathtub her parents had rigged up outside the shack: before the couple installed a bathroom in the main house, a warm bath in winter had meant wading through knee-high snow and pouring boiling water into the tub from a bucket on the woodstove. Candace knew about the shack in the photo, and was aware that it was now vacant, so she suggested that Bella and Philo rent it out to me as a painting retreat.

I was so happy! These folks were very much like my Russian friends: impulsive, adventurous, and passionate. And like Russians in the countryside, they could build anything from scratch. Furthermore, I loved the stark beauty of the Trinity Mountains, and found that my homesickness for Russian dachas vanished in the clear mountain air. And Bella and Philo were delighted that I was putting the empty shack to use.

A year after our marriage, I moved into the shack with all my silk-painting supplies and a tiger-striped cat from Sarah's house, and stayed for a whole month. I spent my painting breaks chopping wood for the old potbellied stove (it was still cold in April), listened to music from a dusty, battery-powered radio, and went to sleep when it got dark. There was no telephone to disturb my concentration, and Tiger stayed inside with me, not wanting to tangle with Bella and Philo's twenty-odd cats, dog, and several goats. The isolation helped me concentrate, and I recaptured my ability to work prolifically and serenely, as I had in the solitude of my dachas.

More than anything else, though, my interlude in Bella and Philo's shack taught me that I could be happy living in the United States: this retreat nurtured me far more than an easy life full of material comforts and an abundance of delicious food. I still missed Russia, but Weaverville was reassuringly like the dacha communities outside Moscow, and here there were even buyers who could afford my paintings. I knew that as long as I could return periodically to the solitude of my mountain hideaway, I would be content. Nevertheless, when I painted and listened to tapes of Russian singers, my old days in Moscow sometimes crowded my head with images.

In Russia, a favorite New Year's Eve tradition was called *"Kalyatki,"* (loosely translated as "Carnival")—Tolstoi colorfully describes it in *War and Peace*. A group of celebrants would dress up in costumes—much like Halloween in America—and knock on people's doors, singing songs, and asking for food and drinks.

I had fallen in love with Carnival since my first experience of it at the Art Insitute, and had organized one in my Moscow studio for twelve years running. Then, after I lost my studio, I decided to have a Carnival party at my winter dacha in Peredelkino. My mother thought I was crazy: the dacha didn't belong to me and people would get drunk, she warned me, and crash through the big windows, or get lost in the dark on their way to the outhouse and poop in the garden. Though I secretly agreed with her, I insisted nothing bad would happen.

The owner gave me permission to have about ten or fifteen people over, but about thirty-five friends showed up. Luckily, they did not break the windows or defile the garden, though they consumed an enormous quantity of vodka. And it was one of the best parties we'd ever had. Everyone rose to to the occasion with outlandish costumes, and we went from house to house, singing and making merry; while Marquise, the enormous resident cat, snored in front of the fire, oblivious to the chaos around him.

Since then, most of the participants had left Russia, and I knew that the ones who remained would probably never be up to that sort of craziness again. So I decided it would be great fun to revive my Carnival tradition in Weaverville on New Year's Eve, and asked Bella and her husband to recruit their friends. Philo, with his experience in theatre, was up for anything that involved getting into a costume, and the two of them agreed.

Steve and I arrived on December thirtieth, but by the morning of the thirty-first we were snowed in by a freak storm that dropped three feet of white stuff on the mountains in twenty-four hours. Our car was completely buried in a drift, and even though we had plenty to eat and drink, Steve, Philo and a neighbor (do boys ever grow up?) decided they would try to clear the road so they could go into town for more beer.

I dressed up in a warm scarf and boots and went out to see the men trying valiantly to move several downed branches from the road. But they kept falling down in the snow and laughing too hard to get up, so I joined them in the drifts, making snow angels and throwing snowballs at them.

Seven hours later, the men returned from town like conquering heroes. Though the power was out all over town, they had found some beer.

Once they had recovered from their exertions, we dressed up, painted our faces like wild

Indians, and went through the woods to a few close neighbors' houses. But I think we made the biggest impression on the next-door-neighbor's geese and donkeys, which began to honk and bray in chorus, drowning out our laughter and songs as we fell in the snow. The more we fell, the more we laughed. And so, in our own silly fashion, we revived Russian Carnival in the California woods.

Though Carnival never took off in Weaverville, the deep drifts of snow connected me with memories of Russia, and the photographs I took provided me with a new set of memories to replace the ones from my Russian life that were fading all too quickly.

Technique

"Winter in Weaverville" embodies the essence of life in the isolated mountain town—its warm, homey interior contrasting with the icicles and gray of a cold winter's day. In this painting, I used the salt technique to create a variety of textural surfaces and to emphasize the different feel between the indoors and the world outside.

There are three glass objects in the painting: the vase, the kerosene lamp, and the bottle. As with the Cliff House painting in the previous chapter, I had to study all the shapes inside the glass and define them very carefully with gutta resist. Then I sprinkled kosher salt on most of the interiors of the glass shapes after the dye was somewhat dry to keep the salt spots more definite.

The smoky, blackened top of the kerosene lamp posed a particular challenge to paint: if I made it very dark, it would look too solid. Fortunately the salt helped open it up to retain an effect of transparency.

For the background outside the window, I wet the entire area between the icicles very liberally, and started to paint while it was still very moist to create the effect of a blurry, frozen world. The extreme wetness allowed me to work, one section at a time, on the areas defined by resist, and still have them look consistent with each other. I applied blue, bits of brown, purple, and black for the tree branches, and added ammonium salt while the painting was still very wet, so it would make very soft marks. The soft, salted background contrasts with the sharper kosher salt spots in the foreground and helps create depth. I also put to work the principle of warm colors in front—cool ones in back.

The only elements in the painting that are not treated with salt are the windowsill, the dark glass with brush and feather, and the shells. Another challenge was the nautilus shell, because the shadow on the round, smooth exterior of the shell had to be placed so that it lay perfectly. Waiting for the precise moment of appropriate dampness allows this to happen.

Winter in Weaverville

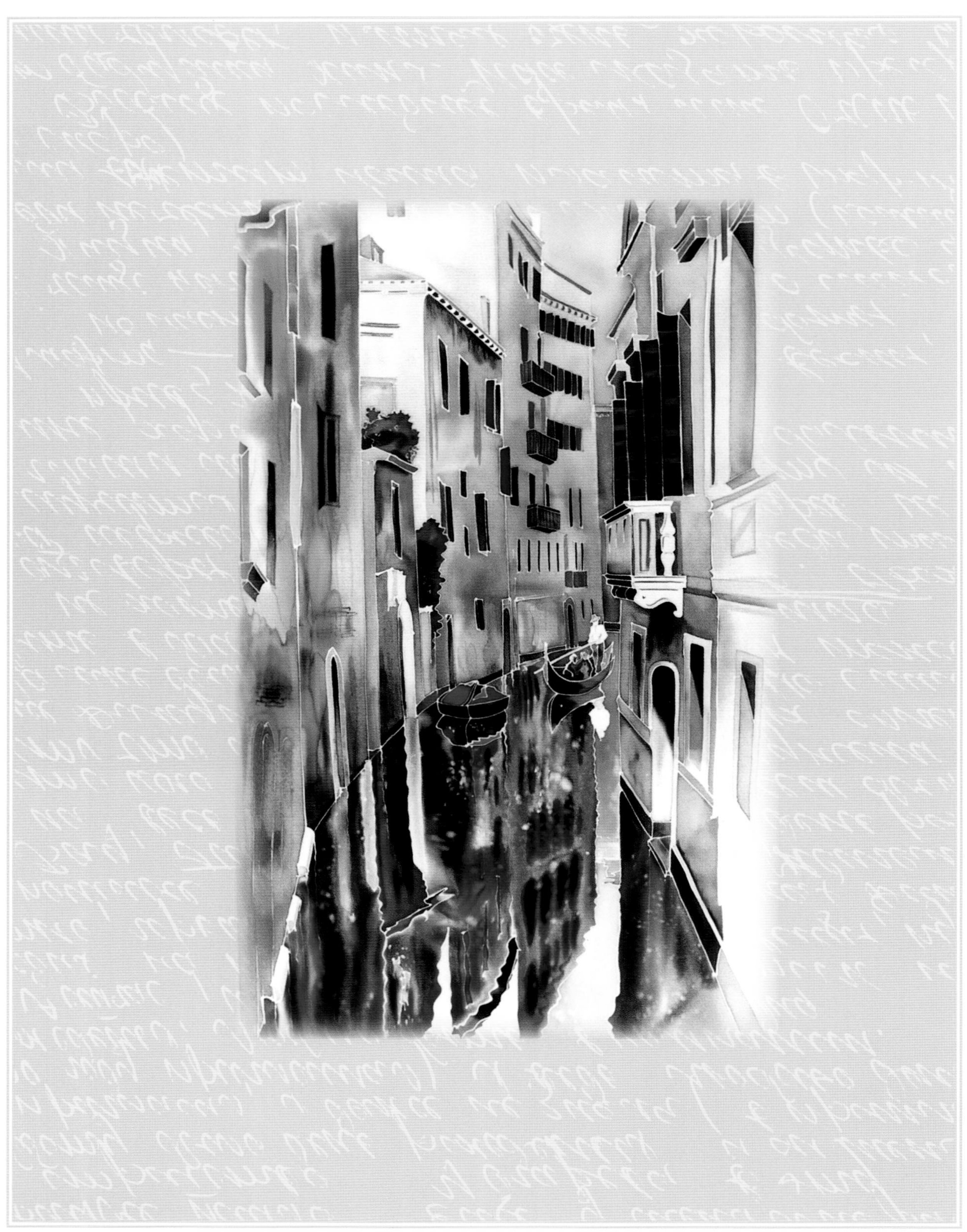

21 Two Suitcases of Gasoline

Maybe it's too early to say, but I don't know if we'll ever again have the opportunity to spend ten weeks in Russia and Europe the way we did in the summer of 1993. Steve and I planned to fly Aeroflot to Moscow, spend two weeks visiting with family and friends, travel for two months in Europe, and then return to Moscow for the flight home. My country was undergoing profound changes, and I had no idea what to expect when we arrived.

I had only been in the States for a little over a year when, in December of 1991, the Soviet Union ceased to exist. The previous August, I had been glued to my television set for days, but the now-famous image of Boris Yeltsin climbing up on a tank in front of thousands of supporters gave little indication of what was really happening. At first, no one could get phone calls through to Moscow, but after weeks of hearing "all circuits busy," I was finally able to reach my mother.

She told me she had been attending meetings, endlessly discussing the future of democracy in our country, and had spent three days protesting in the streets when hard-liners tried to retake the country from Yeltsin and the reformers. But by the time we arrived in Moscow, the euphoria was gone and chaos reigned.

My old familiar boulevards and streets were unrecognizable. Hundreds of kiosks had sprung up at every Metro station and square, selling a jumble of socks, knives, wallets, books, and food. Beautiful young prostitutes walked the streets openly, dressed only in sexy underwear under their coats, and the sleaziest of porno magazines shouted their tawdry delights from newsstands.

What was worse, the wars in Chechnya and Afghanistan had created a human tidal wave of beggars in a capital where public displays of poverty had been forbidden for years. I saw a sleek SUV with darkened windows swerve to keep from running over a legless Soviet soldier on his little wheeled cart, forced to work literally in the lanes of traffic by a mafia gang who would keep most of the wretched veteran's gleanings.

Overwhelmed and saddened by this ugly side of freedom, I was actually relieved to leave for Frankfurt, where we would be staying with a cousin of Steve's who worked for the American military.

With the Russian economy in a shambles—ordinary citizens had lost thousands of dollars in failed banks and pyramid schemes—my mother suggested that Steve and I could buy a used BMW in Germany with some of our money and funds from her almost depleted bank account. By selling the vehicle at a profit back in Moscow, we could make a little money to help her weather the unstable times.

However, we were unaware of the new currency laws that had been enacted to stop capital from flowing out of the former Soviet Union. So when we arrived at the Polish border in Brest, the Russian customs officials took the three thousand dollars we had reserved for the car purchase, handed us a flimsy receipt, and said they would return our money when we came back into Russia. Of course, this was frightening, since it was clear we might never see the cash again, and we had to use a credit card to buy the BMW in Frankfurt. We also bought a gun at the urging of Steve's cousin, because he had heard that traveling in a foreign car in Russia could be very dangerous.

Leaving Frankfurt, we drove the BMW to Switzerland to stay with Sylvia, a beautiful young medical student who had met Steve's cousin Candace in Belgium. From Sylvia's comfortable cottage outside Lucerne, decorated with the bright colors and earthenware pottery she had learned to love while living in Greece, we made day trips into the countryside of Switzerland, enjoying the orderly, tinker-toy villages in valleys dwarfed by snow-topped mountains.

Sylvia was convinced that the elegant black BMW would be stolen in Italy, and said we should travel in her old Ford instead. I called an old friend, Pasha, with whom we would stay in Milan, and he scoffed at the idea that Italy was too crime-ridden for our BMW. But Sylvia and the Ford finally won out, and the three of us took off through the Alps for the spectacular mountain lakes of northern Italy, and subsequently arrived in Milan.

Ironically, a friend came to meet us on our first night at Pasha's apartment, and his own brand-new BMW was stolen from Pasha's driveway as we lay sleeping. Suddenly, the Ford looked very good to us.

From Milan, we drove down the western coast of Italy, taking in Genoa, then the Cinqueterra region and La Spezia. Sylvia had lived several years in Florence, and had very good friends there—a family who owned a vineyard. So we were able to stay in Florence for a whole week with them. The splendid city was virtually an art museum, and like most visitors, we tried to see as much as possible during our short stay. Sylvia took a train back to Switzerland, and Steve and I continued on to Siena.

When we stepped into our hotel room, I thought I saw a beautiful painting on the wall; it took several seconds for me to realize that the painting was a window that was framing our view of the city. We decided not to go out for dinner, but bought some antipasto, bread, and a bottle of Chianti, so we could sit by the window and inhale the scene. Siena's buildings were all constructed from the raw, earthy, red-brown stone that gives the paint color "burnt sienna" its name, and I loved the tonal unity of the churches and buildings surrounding the horseshoe-shaped plaza.

Of course, we visited all the well-known tourist spots like Pisa and Lucca, but the most enjoyable part of our trip was just driving around the Tuscan countryside, finding unexpected treasures in little towns off the beaten path: an ancient fountain by the side of the road, Etruscan ruins on a lonely hillside.

After returning from my cruise out of Odessa, I had taken Italian lessons in Moscow, because I dreamed of returning to Italy and seeing Venice. But the actual city outdid all my expectations.

Even though it was crammed to the bursting point with tourists, Venice succeeded in charming us. We found a room with a great view right on the Grand Canal next to the Piazza San Marco, not knowing that Venice never sleeps, and the boat traffic was as noisy as a freeway almost all night.

I got up each morning at five, before the city became jammed with people. Stalking the empty streets with my camera, I took hundreds of shots of the timeworn buildings as the colors of their facades changed subtly over two hours of gradual sunrise—with only me, the cats, and the pigeons enjoying it all.

Venice remains the most enchanting place for me to paint—it is still the city that most feeds my imagination. After several visits, I have created over forty paintings from my photographs, and there will certainly be more. I love the city's faded elegance and air of romance, and its vignettes of architectural beauty at every turn of the narrow, twisting streets. And for me, the reflections in water everywhere make Venice an artist's heaven on earth.

As we were driving back from Milan to Switzerland to return Sylvia's borrowed Ford, we remembered that she had asked us to buy a quantity of Italian wine and olive oil, since everything was four times more expensive in the tidy Swiss cantons. But every large market in Como, the last city of size before the border, was closed for an Italian national holiday, so we began scouring the neighborhoods for the little family shops that had remained open. The phone lines must have crackled with activity, because the owners were waiting for us in their doorways when we pulled up.

By the time we had finished Sylvia's shopping list, the Ford was stuffed so full of bottles that we looked like itinerant olive-oil peddlers. Noting our Lucerne license plates, some Swiss people stopped to chat with their fellow countrymen, only to find the Ford occupied by a Russian and an American. The serious-minded Swiss must have thought they had interrupted some sort of cold-war escapade. But even with high duties at the border, Sylvia still came out ahead.

Loading up the black BMW for our return trip to Moscow, we planned to make a beeline for Brest, where we were to cross back into Russia, because our visas were expiring. We enjoyed a brief stay in Warsaw, including a dinner with Candace, who was in town for a midwives' conference, and regaled her with our impressions of Italy. Then we were off.

But our mad dash to the border was brought to a complete halt before we even got to Brest: the backup of cars was literally a mile long. And when someone offered to sell us his place in line for two hundred dollars, we couldn't accept, since our money was still in the hands of the Russian officials. So we sat in the car all night, dozing on and off, and worrying that we would be searched and arrested for carrying a weapon: Steve had hidden our gun in one of his boots and the bullets in the other one.

Twenty-four hours later, when we finally reached the front of the line, the guard tried everything to harass us: Americans were not allowed to bring a foreign car into Russia, and our visas were invalid as we had showed up two days later than the stamped date. We protested that we had followed the regulations and telegraphed ahead that we would be late, but he just shrugged. Of course all of this was the guard's attempt to weasel a bribe from us, and he pompously declared that "as a representative of the Belarussian government," he would allow us through for four hundred dollars. I indicated that we'd be glad to oblige if he'd hand over the three thousand dollars that had been taken from us at the border earlier; but he said that he would have to talk with his supervisors, and disappeared at around dusk with both our passports. We spent another horribly anxious night, watching other people getting searched; but when the guard showed up in the morning, he inexplicably grunted that we could pass.

Our ordeal was not over, however, since we still had to go through customs. By this time, so many people were going over the border that the government had turned the central railway station outside Brest into a giant customs agency. Though we were weak and exhausted after two nights at the border without sleep, we had no other choice.

The chaotic economic conditions had created a new class of people, called *chelnok* (in Russian literally "back and forth") who made money by trading goods between Russia and Poland. A sea of travelers waited beside stacks of bags and boxes that needed to be checked for contraband. The stench of unwashed bodies and urine almost knocked me over, since my Americanized nose had forgotten the smell of a Russian train station. I couldn't even use the pay toilets, as I had no ruble coins in my wallet.

In tears, I went outside to call my mother with a phone card I found in one of my pockets. But when my grandmother answered, she said that my mother had taken the train to meet us in Brest: when I telegraphed the Brest customs agency to advise them that we would arrive after our visas had expired, I had also sent one to my mother, so she knew when we would arrive at the train station.

I found Steve sitting on a bench in the square, unshaven and bedraggled. Seeing his black mustache and hearing his bad accent as he mumbled the one phrase he had memorized—"I don't understand Russian"—two drunks had become convinced he was a Georgian pretending not to speak Russian, and they were now badgering him to go in with them on a bottle of vodka. I drove them off with a barrage of Russian insults.

Fueled by my anger at the drunks, I stormed back into the train station and made a football rush for the customs window, using sleeping bodies as stepping-stones to get through the jam of boxes and travelers. Bony hands reached out to stop me like some scene in a horror movie. At the window, I asked for my money, but an underling pretended not to know what I was talking about, and the woman in charge had the day off. At that point, I lost it completely and began a screaming, tearful, tirade, demanding that the stunned clerk hand over my cash. She walked away, and miraculously returned five minutes later, thrusting our three thousand dollars and a signed customs slip into my hand.

Outside once more, I ran into my mother in a crowd next to the train station. *Why does she have two huge suitcases, so heavy she can barely balance them?* I wondered.

She explained that while we were in Europe, she had been reading in the papers that the Brest-Moscow highway had become extremely dangerous. No gas was available, so people by the side of road would offer to sell drivers a container or two, and then their accomplices hiding in the woods would spring out and rob the buyers, sometimes even killing them and stealing their cars. So my mother had bought two twenty-liter cans of gasoline, wrapped them in blankets in two suitcases, and illegally smuggled the highly explosive liquids onto the train. For the next several weeks, scary images haunted my thoughts: the train exploding into flames, or my mother locked in a prison cell as a punishment for her crime.

The road back to Moscow was deserted, and badly in need of repair. Of course there were no rest stops—only an occasional well where we could splash our faces with a dipper of cold water. The villages seemed abandoned, and the only people we saw were the Russian police who kept stopping our car and asking for our papers.

With the central government's presence in the countryside now almost nonexistent, the only source of income for the locals was handing out speeding tickets, and we got several of them. However, the ruble had been devaluated so much that the fine for speeding was now seven hundred rubles (about one U.S. dollar), and since the out-of-date Soviet-era tickets still showed a five-ruble fine, each ticket was a clumsy two-inch stack of papers. Steve still keeps them all in a closet somewhere as a memento of our hair-raising journey.

Exhausted, we desperately needed to rest, so we stopped before reaching Kiev and staggered out of the car. Steve and I slept on the gasoline-scented blankets on the grass by the road, while my mother sat vigil, holding the gun to guard us while we grabbed a few hours sleep.

Back in Moscow, my friends were horrified to see the black BMW. We couldn't have known it, but this car had become the favorite choice of Chechen gangsters. Sure enough, I spied four of them the next day, riding around in a new, leather-upholstered black BMW with the sun roof open in the pouring rain, just to make Chechens without a sunroof crazy with jealousy.

Rather than risk our lives trying to sell the BMW at the flea market, I contacted a friend with black-market connections, and he arranged for the ill-fated car to be sold for about the same price we had paid in Germany. But we didn't care about the investment any more, since we were all still alive.

Before we returned to California, I wanted Steve to see Suzdal. It was my Russian touchstone, and I also wanted us to have shared memories of the town's serene meadows, churches, and ancient monastery walls.

Technique

When I come back from a trip with hundreds of photographs, I notice that the pictures I have taken with the architecture in focus usually have a sky that is blurry, whitish gray, or completely blue. But in a silk painting, a big stretch of blue just looks like blue fabric. So I am always on the lookout for a good sky, and when I see one, I photograph it. My favorites are the ones before a storm, rainy or winter skies, cloudy sunsets, and colorful sunrises.

Before starting a painting, I go through my sky pictures and find one that suits it perfectly. In "Venice, View from Plaza San Marco," I chose a sky photo with the yellowish-grays of an oncoming storm, to match the color tones of the buildings.

When I paint a sky, I usually wet the entire area first with clear water, because whatever I paint will have to be soft-edged. And for added softness, I paint the area a little sooner than I would paint a face. For "Venice, View from Plaza San Marco," I mixed my sky gray from a little black, a touch of blue, and a spot of yellow, leaving some areas almost white to indicate the upper parts of the clouds. Then I took a tiny bit of darkish-blue or purple and rubbed it into the undersides of the clouds with a semi-dry brush to create their shadows.

Sometimes, the colors are not dark enough when the sky dries, and I have to wet the area again and add more color. But the effect is always better if I do it in one pass.

In this painting, there are several areas where I put the technique of layering to good use. Many silk painters find that the white lines of the gutta resist create an effect that is too cartoon-like and unnatural. For example, there isn't a single white resist line in the dark blue, arched structure on the left.

First I painted the whole area a medium blue. After the blue dried, I outlined with resist the areas I wanted to keep in the medium blue. Then I painted another set of features in a darker blue (over the original blue) and let them dry. After delineating another set of resist lines, I added more color in several successive stages, until I finally painted the underside of the arches black. On the clay-colored bell tower, as well as on on the gray building with the tall columns on the far right, I used the same technique.

To create two different effects, I also sprinkled two types of salt on areas of this painting while they were still wet: ammonium salt for the water, and sea salt for the paving stones of the piazza. And I muted and toned down all the colors to give the feeling of wet pavements and buildings.

Venice, View from Plaza San Marco

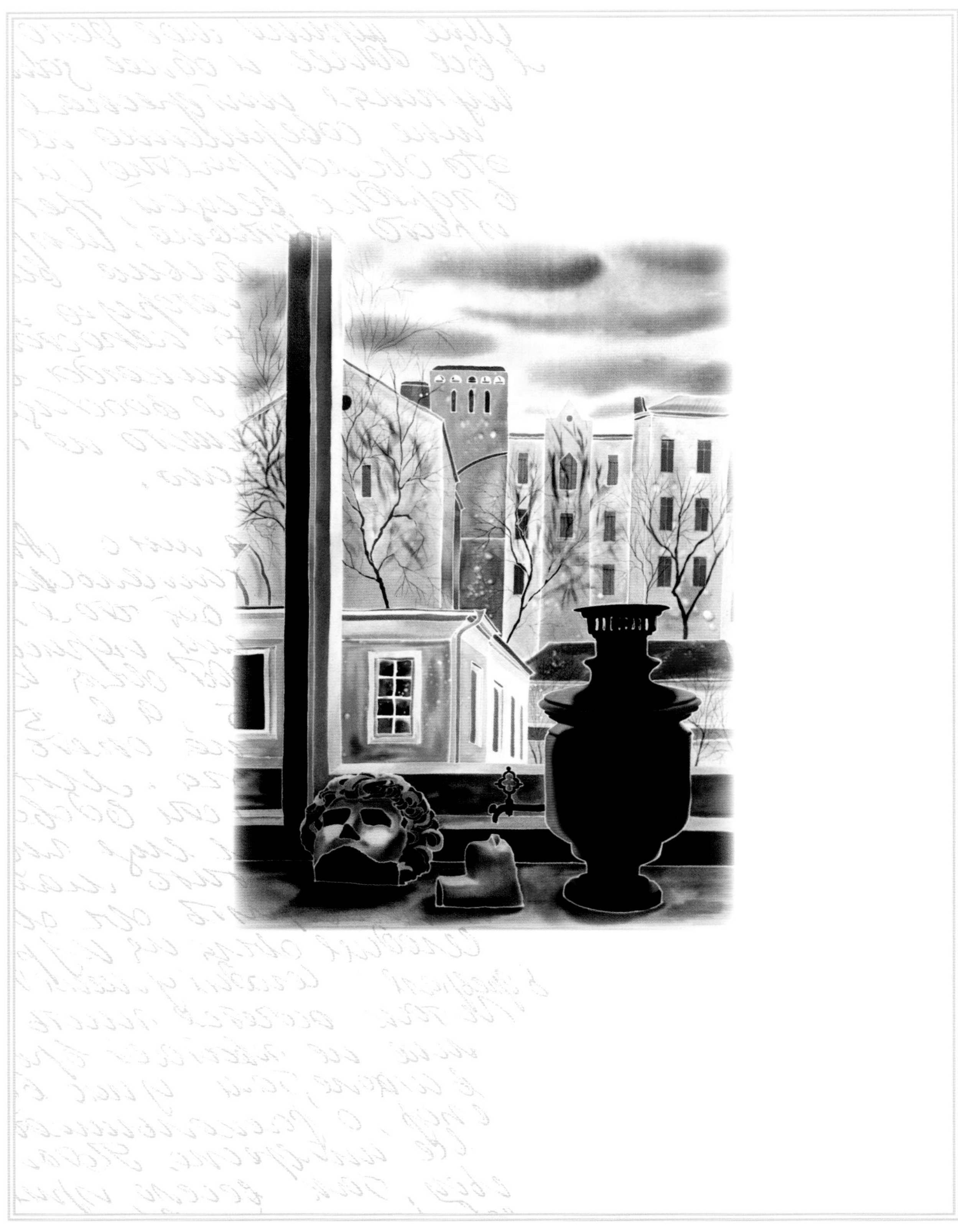

22 Between Two Worlds

All of my friend Misha's documents, including his driver's license, had been stolen when he turned away from his briefcase for a minute at a sidewalk restaurant, and he couldn't drive anywhere legally. So just before Steve and I delivered the BMW to its new owners, we took him on a trip to Suzdal in the relative comfort of the luxury car. Kolya, a mutual friend, made it a foursome.

While Steve navigated the narrow highway linking Moscow to the medieval town, the three Russians opened a bottle of vodka to celebrate anything we could think of: our marriage, Steve's first visit, and Misha's escape from his law office. Soon we were in pretty high spirits, and Misha asked, "What do we have here—an American driving three drunk Russians to Suzdal?" Steve shouted, "It's humanitarian aid!" and was greeted with gales of appreciative laughter.

That May was unseasonably cold, and it even started to snow. So for about fifty cents, Steve bought a blue wool coat in a second-hand store. The sturdy, old-fashioned worker's garment would have been boring to any style-conscious New Russian, but Steve loved it. With his travel-worn, unshaven face, and his eyes bleary from the unaccustomed rounds of vodka shots, Steve easily passed for a local Russian.

One evening, as we walked along the old earthwork defense ramparts, we were welcomed into a circle of local men keeping warm around a bonfire. Whenever they addressed Steve during their lively, engaging chatter, he just nodded, so at one point the men asked me what was wrong with my fellow. I admitted that he was my American husband who didn't understand Russian, and the locals were astonished: Steve was the first foreigner they had ever met.

Before Western tourists started coming to Russia in any numbers, Russians excitedly welcomed the rare foreign visitors with gifts, no matter how little they had to offer. So one of the men ran into a nearby house and brought out the finest treasures he could lay hands on: a bottle of vodka and a bowl full of *xolodiets*, a rich chicken broth without the fat skimmed off, poured over some slivers of chicken, and then frozen. It looked like a quivering bowl of greasy jello, and Steve couldn't hide the horror in his face when he tried to swallow a bite of the slithery mess. So I made excuses for him, saying he was getting over the flu and didn't have much of an appetite.

For the next few days, our new Suzdal buddies took us around town, and introduced us to their friends, one of whom was the local history teacher. Unable to survive on his wretched government salary, he was growing cucumbers in the large walled garden of an old house he had bought and renovated, right next to one of Suzdal's loveliest churches.

In the late afternoon, when the teacher took us to the Museum of Wooden Architecture, the place was deserted except for the attendants in period costume. These old women huddled together stoically in the unseasonably cold rooms that could not be heated because of the ancient materials.

We felt sorry for the shivering old babushkas, and ran back to a little shop and bought them a bottle of vodka. Surprised and pleased, they brought out some simple piroshkis and black bread, and we all sat in one of the wooden houses and shared a meal together. I don't know how we survived the cheap, unfiltered vodka, but they so enjoyed telling us their stories that it was worth losing a few more brain cells.

Steve flew home while I stayed for three more weeks in Moscow, visiting everyone in my worn address book. But I wasn't really part of their Russian lives any more, and most of them were too busy surviving to give me much attention. It was very painful to feel shut out, because it was, after all, my beloved country: I had lived there for twenty-eight years, and I had many good memories. But like the Aeroflot plane on my return to California, flying thousands of feet above the earth's surface, I now floated between two worlds, not really belonging to one or the other—as rootless as the clouds that hung suspended outside the plane's window.

Soon after my return, I began a campaign to convince Steve that we should have a child. He had a lot of reservations, saying that perhaps our nervous systems wouldn't be able to handle being parents since we weren't so young and resilient anymore. But I just felt it was the right time: I had always wanted to experience motherhood, and my recent visits with my Russian friends had reminded me how quickly our lives were passing.

In the autumn of 1994, I became pregnant. After the first few months of very bad morning sickness, I recovered, and I was able to paint on silk throughout my pregnancy. But the psychological changes I was experiencing were even more significant than the physical ones.

For most of my life, I had been sure that I would die young. There was nothing in my Russian experience that allowed me to imagine I might live long enough to enjoy a peaceful retirement and old age. I lived, ate, and drank as if there were no tomorrow, since the future held no certainties.

Now, for the first time, I could look forward to decent health care, relatively inexpensive and readily available food, and a mild climate where I could exercise and swim outdoors almost the year round. What's more, I could afford to provide all the material needs of the child growing inside me, and could reasonably expect to be the grandmother of my baby's children.

This realization was an all-important milestone, and everything changed because of it. I stopped drinking alcohol entirely, took the best prenatal vitamins, and ate the freshest, healthiest food whenever possible.

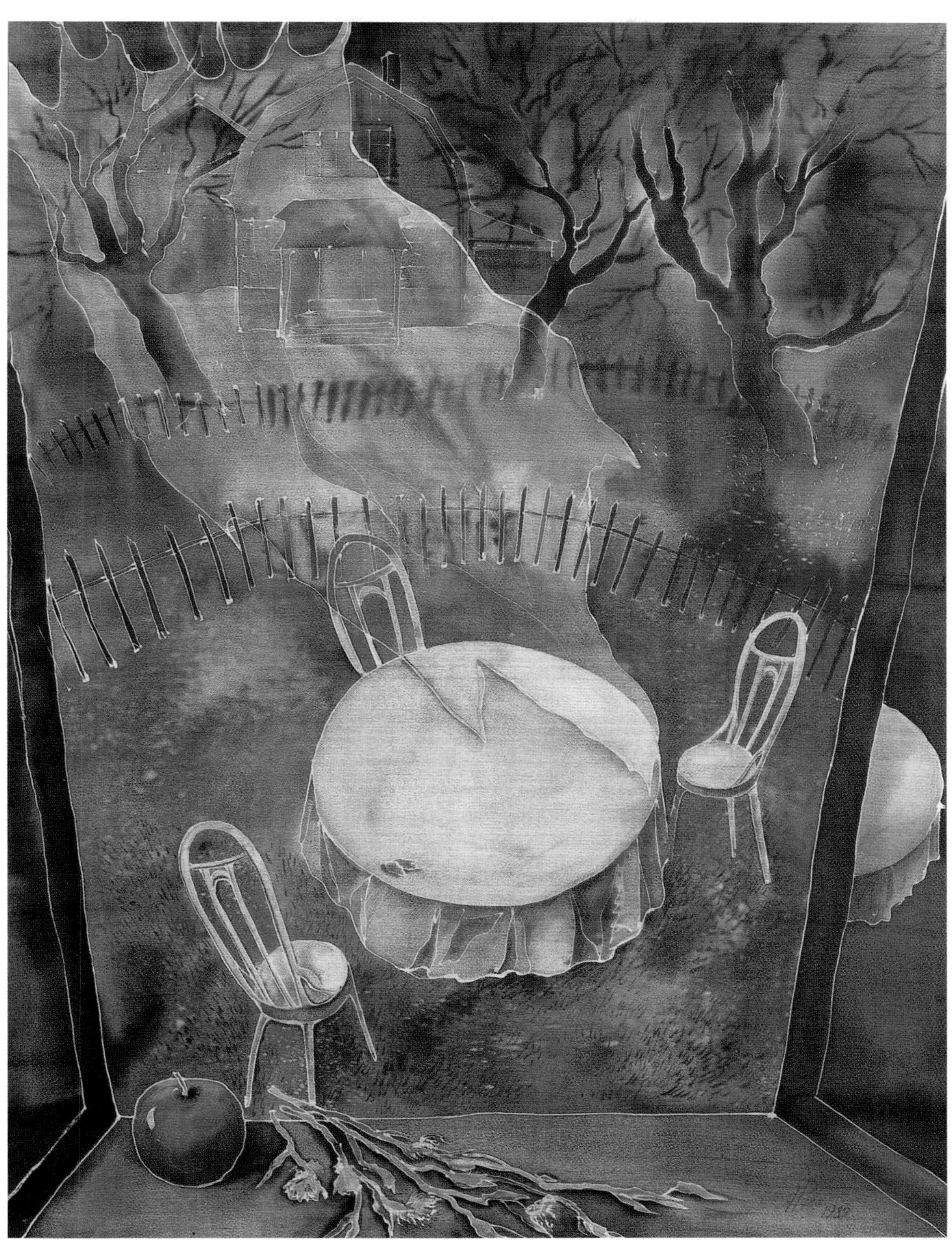

Summer Evening

We knew that after our baby started walking, I wouldn't be able to paint on the dining-room table any more, with jars of dye everywhere waiting to be spilled by little hands. So Steve began building a studio for me in our attic. Now I would be able to paint with a stunning view of San Francisco Bay outside my window, and I would finally have the location for my studio that I had dreamed of all my life: on the top floor, with my creative mind directly connected to the stars, and without the auras of other people breaking the energy field.

During my seventh month, I flew to Holland, where I had been invited to hang a show of my silk paintings at the Silk Museum in Wouw. The show was very successful, but the reception was ghastly for me: almost everyone there chain-smoked, and I felt very ill.

In general, though, I was still strong, and worked on my silk paintings until three days before I went into labor. It was a pretty hard labor, but I didn't ask for any painkillers. Our baby boy was a big guy: nine pounds and twelve ounces. We named him Misha after my grandfather, and Steve put the final touches on the studio the week I came home from the hospital.

Months earlier, I had signed up to teach children the art of painting on silk at the Jewish Community Center summer camp in Palo Alto. Unfortunately, the session started when Misha was only two weeks old. Luckily for me, my mother had finally decided to leave Russia—it had become too difficult—and live near us in San Francisco. When Misha was born, she was glad to be the doting grandmother and help with her first (and maybe only) grandchild. I was thankful when she took care of Misha in between feedings while I taught the kids.

Even with my busy life and the joy of watching my son grow, I still missed my friends terribly—our crazy costumed art-studio parties and kitchen-table conversations—and simply speaking in my own language. So I decided to go back to Moscow: either I would find some relief from my homesickness, or discover that I didn't really need Russia any more. Misha was now almost two and a half, and I could leave him with my mother and Steve in San Francisco.

I arrived in September of 1997, expecting to enjoy the two weeks of sunshine that Russians call "women's summer." I hoped to paint the brilliant oranges and reds of fall foliage against the white of birch tree trunks, but it wasn't to be, since it rained almost every day I was there. And I was very depressed at what I saw: Russia and I were like two trains speeding by each other in opposite directions.

Moscow was even more unrecognizable that it had been in the chaotic days of my trip in 1993. My home town had become the International Capital of Making Money: the familiar spaces for art exhibitions now housed commercial trade shows that sold espresso machines and knock-offs of Louis Vuitton handbags. Moreover, the majority of my friends had lost their jobs as the economy sputtered; some even had to give up their Moscow apartments and were camping out at their dachas in very reduced circumstances.

Misha offered to cheer me up with a trip to Suzdal, but it was the first time my peaceful refuge let me down. Now that Russians could take affordable trips to Turkey and Spain, they had deserted the old Russian towns like Suzdal, and Misha and I were the only guests in a hotel with rooms for over two hundred people. Our friend from the previous trip, the local history teacher, had stopped growing cucumbers; his life had lost all sense of order, he was drinking heavily, and he was deeply depressed.

I took a train to St. Petersburg, and the three days there helped to wipe out the sadness of the rest of the trip. Perhaps it was because I had never lived there, and the changes didn't hurt as personally as those in Moscow.

On a gloriously sunny day, when I was taking photos at Pushkin, my favorite palace, I ran into a young student who had lived in the Bay Area briefly, then moved back to St. Petersburg. She told me about some artists she'd like me to meet; so the next day, when the chilly autumn rain returned, we bought a bottle of vodka for her pals and set out to visit them.

Facing the Fontanka River, the studio windows revealed a typically wet, gray, St. Petersburg day. The setting brought back the days of my youth—those years full of great friends, drinking, and talking about art. I did a painting from a photograph of one window, and every Russian who sees it recognizes the familiar scene instantaneously: the materially poor but creatively rich life of the artist, living from day to day on a big pot of soup and a bottle of vodka. Nostalgia for the old days tugged at my heart, yet sadness at my friends' situations pulled me back to thoughts of my life in California, where I wouldn't constantly be reminded that they were falling apart. When I returned to the States, however, I still felt pulled in two directions.

By Misha's seventh year, he began to question why I often spoke to him in Russian. I had always wanted him to be able to speak fluently in my native tongue, and I thought he was old enough now for a visit to Russia, where he would begin to understand our shared heritage.

My art-collector friend, Audrey, had been talking about a trip to Russia for several years, since she wanted to explore her Russian-Jewish heritage. And Jeanne-Michele, the co-author of this book, wanted to experience Russia first-hand. Since Jeanne-Michele and Audrey would be traveling companions, I arranged for them to rent a central Moscow apartment from a friend's ex-mother-in-law. Zoya would help them orient themselves to the city while Steve and I introduced our boy to friends and family.

I would also have a show of my work in Moscow. Michael Katz, the owner of Rupert, Gibbon & Spider, a prominent supplier of silk dyes, was hosting one of his Russian customers, and he asked me to show them around San Francisco. Since the visitors didn't know anyone else in the city, they stayed with Steve and me, and I took them to several Russian parties. They were very grateful, and so they offered to organize the show for me in Moscow, using their connections at the Central Hall of Artists in Moscow's prestigious State Art Gallery. Michael asked me to demonstrate his Jacquard Red Label dyes at the show as well.

Unfortunately, this trip, too, was plagued with difficulties. I had a horrible stomach flu the first few days in Moscow, and not only was it the hottest summer in years, but huge peat fires were also burning underground on the outskirts of the city. A pall of smoke hung over everything, day and night, making it very hard to breathe. Everyone who could leave Moscow did, and if it hadn't been for the show, we would have retreated as well.

Because of the heat wave, loyal friends and relatives were almost the only people who attended my show. But since so many of my closest companions had left Russia for new lives in Europe and the States, my connections to those who did come were not very strong. What's more, I was the only sober person in the crowd, and felt that I just didn't belong anymore.

Right after the show, Misha, little Misha, Steve, and I left for Suzdal, where we could all cool off in the river. The town had been cleaned up and revitalized, and we got directions in the marketplace to rooms for rent in the newly constructed home of an army retiree. Vadim Yurovich was pretty much a drunk, but he held things together somehow, with the help of a slightly less potted bodyguard-handyman, and his price was reasonable.

However, earlier that week in Moscow some nasty insect had bitten me, and my leg was so painfully swollen I could barely walk. Vadim had connections at the local hospital, but the small clinic reminded me all too vividly of my past liver infection: it was a shabby place, with something horridly green and slimy dripping down the walls. I was worried that the doctor would be as drunk as Vadim, but he was quite competent, even though the huge tufts of hair sprouting from his ears gave him a comic look. Thankfully, the doctor gave me some antibiotics and a special wrap for my leg.

When a friend in St. Petersburg invited us to spend the following weekend on a sailing yacht, we were happy to accept, and most eager for a pleasant end to our journey. The train trip to St. Petersburg was fun for Misha, and I was able to take several rolls of photos in the city to inspire future paintings.

We arrived at the yacht club toting beer for Steve and plenty of vodka for the boat's owner (Lyuba said that he would welcome any guests who provided the drinks.) The captain soon introduced us to the local sailing traditions on the Gulf of Finland—we were to greet Buoy 25 with a round of vodka shots, and the same at Buoy 30 and a string of others. At Buoy 40 we discovered a boatload of the captain's friends who hopped onto our boat armed with food and drinks, ready to party.

I hadn't warned Steve that for about five hundred years, Russians had been enjoying the sport of encouraging foreign visitors to become helplessly drunk. And when everyone shouted the traditional Russian saying, "Drinking vodka without beer is like throwing money into the wind!" Steve forgot about the intense sun and the waves and took the admonition literally, chasing the vodka shots with suds. By the time we reached a little rocky island to enjoy a swim in the bay, he was fast asleep below-decks.

Only one tie-up was available on the island—a metal bridge over a small inlet—so we lashed our boat to another family's; they were already on the island and waved us their permission. Misha went off to clamber about on a lookout tower with a girl his age from the other boat, and the family, noticing our lack of provisions, invited us to help them barbecue the bucket of fish they had caught.

Happily sitting on the rocks in the midsummer evening light, my belly full of delicious fish and the island's berries, I saw Steve emerge from below and try to bridge the gap between the two tied-up boats, now swaying and dipping in a brisk evening wind. Fully dressed, he flopped into the water and came up sputtering—and without his prescription sunglasses. It would have been hilarious, except that he cut his fingers quite badly. The woman from the other sailboat improvised a bandage for him from strips of her white shirt. Our captain, who had by now imbibed enough vodka to stun a rhinoceros, dove into the water, and after several tries, came up triumphantly with the expensive glasses in his hand.

Later Steve would joke that "someone came up with the idea of holding 'extreme' sporting events, but Russians definitely have the corner on 'extreme' vacationing. . ."

I couldn't blame my friends and acquaintances, as they were very dear to me, and I understood that the drinking was their way of coping with the stresses of everyday life in Russia. But when I saw them disintegrating, losing their teeth and in poor health, it made me sadder than anything else in my entire life.

All in all, it was the most trying and difficult trip I had ever taken, and the state of my friends left me quite depressed for several months afterward: the rash of illnesses and injuries seemed like some sort of sign. I wasn't sure I would ever return to Russia again.

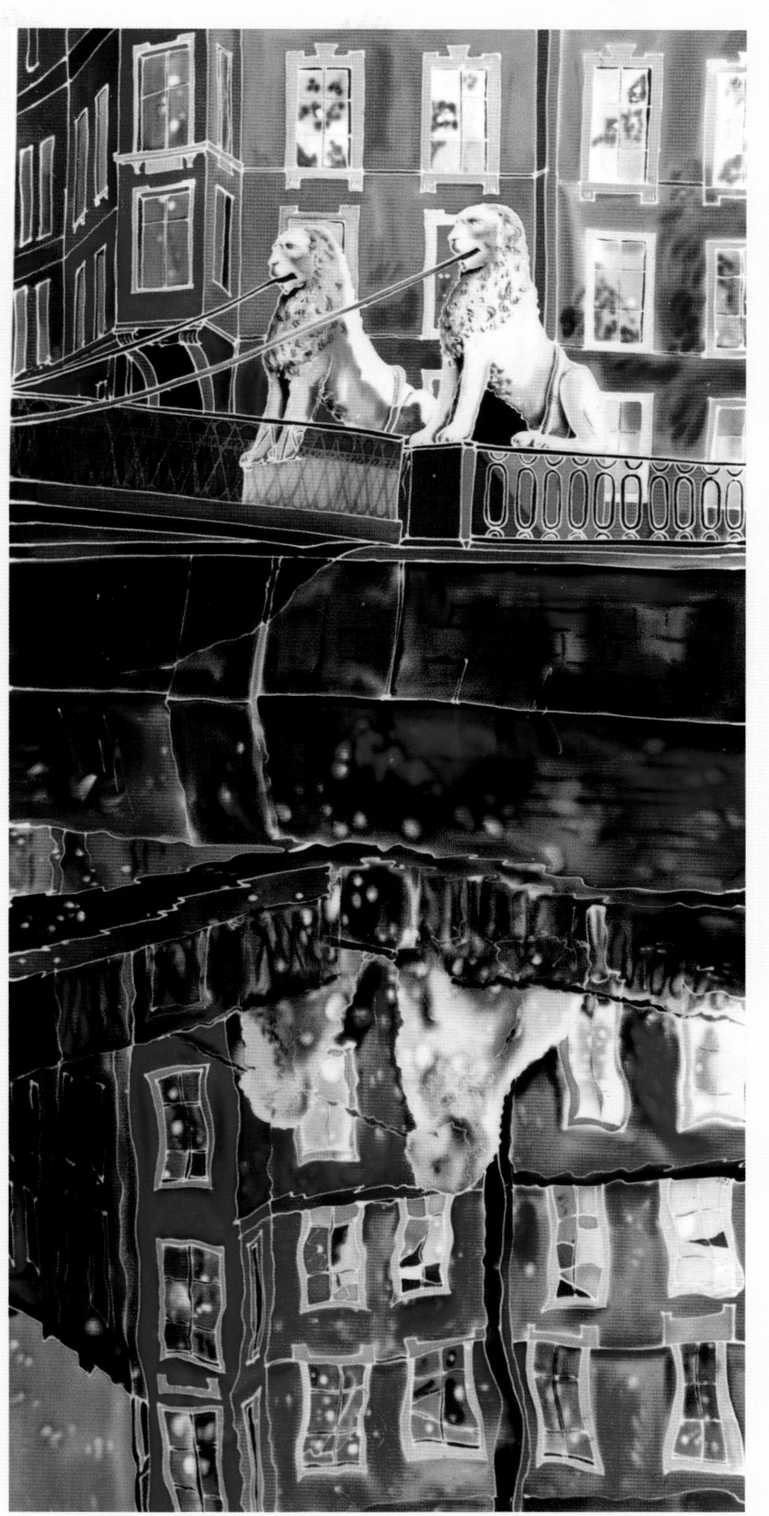

Technique

The painting "St. Petersburg, the Artists' Studio" is all about the contrast between the objects in the foreground and the scene behind them.

I delineated the foreground objects with gutta resist directly onto the white silk, so that the contrast between the white lines and the painted shapes would bring them closer to the viewer. To show that the spoon was made of metal, I wet the whole spoon area, then kept a strong contrast between the yellow highlight bordered with blue, and the white highlight down the middle of the spoon.

For the lid of the stock pot, I painted the various shapes in high contrast, almost black and white, to show that it was made of a shiny metal. Painting most of the lid in a very pale color, I waited until it was dry, then I added little shapes of a slightly darker blue-gray to show that the surface was not completely smooth. I also outlined in resist the shadow of the spoon on the lid to create a sharp edge, and made it follow the curved shape of the lid.

I wanted the background to have entirely the opposite effect, so I first painted it with a blue-gray hue. Then I painted all the resist lines on top of the initial color after it was dry, so that when I added more color, the resist lines would appear blue-gray and cause the background to recede. I used only pastel tones, worked very wet, and added lots of salt to indicate the rainy, overcast day.

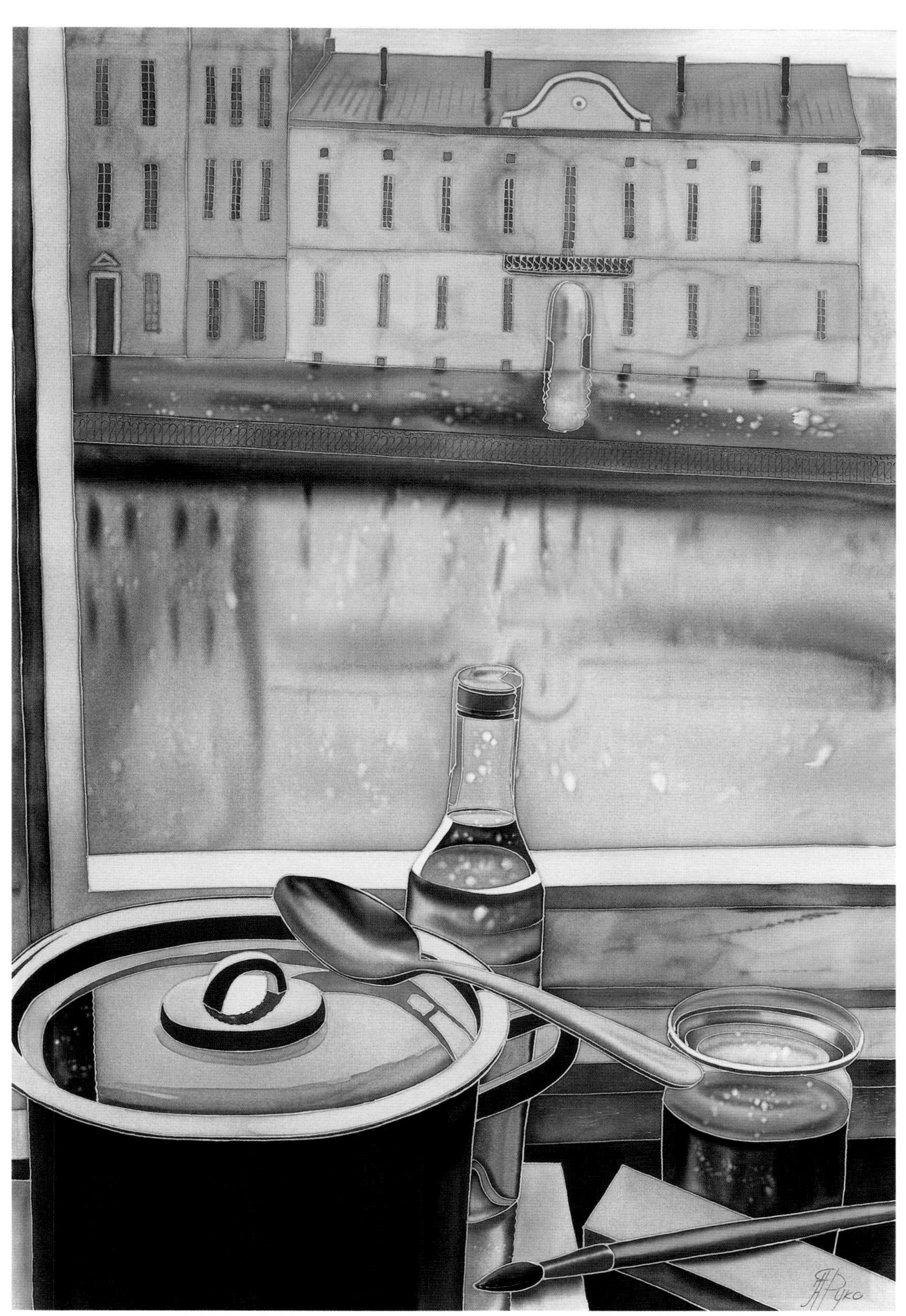

St. Petersburg, the Artists' Studio

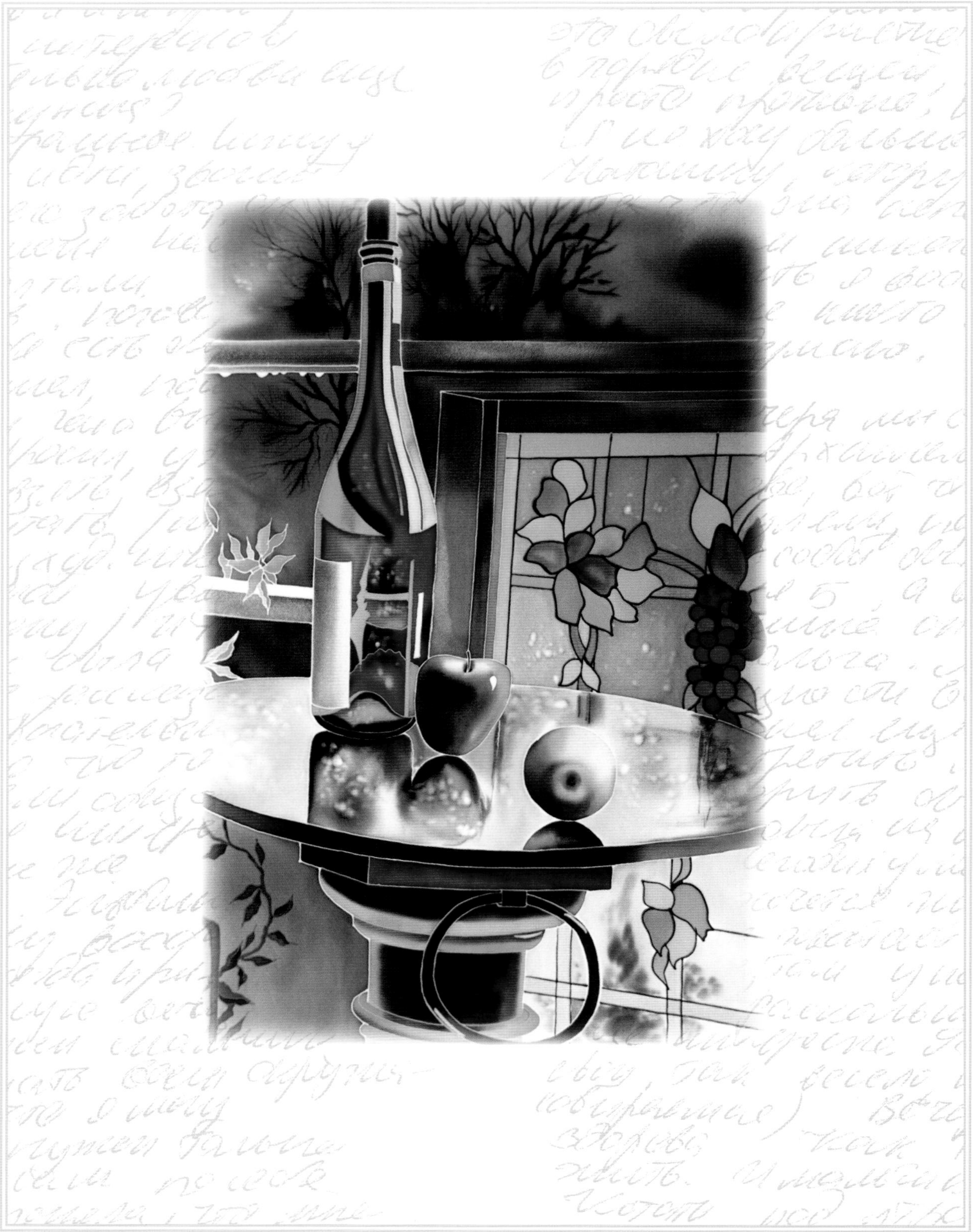

23 Mendocino

Shortly after Steve and I were married, Bella introduced me to the owner of the Bill Zimmer Gallery in Mendocino, a picturesque coastal community four hours' drive north of San Francisco. Bill loved my work, and invited me to display a group of my paintings in his gallery in November of 1992.

Mendocino's remoteness has kept it small, and strong preservation standards protect its historic character. At first a back-to-the-land outpost for sixties-era hippies escaping from the squalor of urban communes, it is now a viable artistic community, with shops, galleries, and elegant bed-and-breakfast accommodations. When I first saw the little town perched on cliffs above the azure sea, I fell in love: the clusters of old wooden buildings and churches felt like Suzdal, with its peaceful, healing atmosphere.

The narrow two-lane highway to the Mendocino coast passes through the Jackson State Forest, a wild expanse laced with a network of unpaved roads. Steve loves to explore, so on our first trip to deliver my paintings to the gallery, we took off randomly down a nameless track. For me, it was pleasantly similar to a Russian forest—no signs, no people, and no campgrounds. After about an hour of aimless driving, I started to notice what appeared to be big mushrooms on the side of road, so I asked Steve to stop the car. When I looked closer, I immediately recognized the rounded, orange-capped shapes as the prized fungi that we Russians call "white mushrooms."

Now it must be understood that mushroom hunting has always been a national sport in Russia—a feverish passion bordering on obsession. Every summer, the woods and forests are often filled with more mushroom pickers than actual mushrooms, which are treasures so tasty and nutritious that people dry, salt, and pickle every precious morsel to enhance monotonous winter meals. Mushrooming holds our Russian identity as strongly as caviar or the Kremlin.

As we walked a few steps further into the Mendocino woods, we found a huge stand of the big, edible beauties, which I later learned were called "Manzanita Boletus."

Only once before in my life had I found so many mushrooms: I was about four years old,

traveling with my grandparents, when we came across a similar woodland scene. Half-covered by the green fronds of lacy ferns, as if fairies has hidden them there for me, were dozens and dozens of the hugest mushrooms I had ever seen.

The memory of that discovery was so strong that it had become a life-long recurring dream, and this Jackson Forest experience was like the dream come true. Besides, I didn't expect to find mushrooms in November at all, so our find was even more serendipitous. Steve and I picked several large bags full, and found out later that it was an unusually productive season, with an abundance rarely seen by the locals.

During this same time period, Susan Moyer, the author of *Silk Painting: The Artist's Guide to Gutta and Wax Resist Techniques*, was teaching at the Mendocino Art Center, and after seeing my paintings at the Bill Zimmer Gallery, she wanted to include some of my images in her second book, *Silk Painting for Fashion and Fine Art*. It was a great opportunity for me to get wider exposure for my work, and with Susan's recommendation, I started teaching classes at the Art Center.

My first two-day class was a success, and the staff asked me when I would like to come back and teach for five days. "November!" the mushroom enthusiast in me immediately answered.

For several autumns thereafter, I combined precious hours picking mushrooms in the forest—alone or with Steve and Misha—with the intensely creative environment of a group of silk artists, usually women, each student bringing her energy and artistic vision to the five-day sessions.

Of course I shared my enthusiasm for mushrooms with my students, and after they presented me with a beautiful cookbook on preparing wild mushrooms, I invited them all to my rooms, where I cooked up a Boletus feast heavy with the aromas of garlic and Madeira wine. Some students waited for a few hours before trying the dish to see if I was going to die, but after a while, they realized that all wild mushrooms weren't dangerous if they were carefully chosen by an experienced hunter. There is a saying, "There are old mushroom hunters, and bold ones, but there are no old and bold mushroom hunters," and I fully intended to be an old one.

Every evening, we'd enjoy a potluck dinner in one of the cottages the students had rented, share great meals and wine, set up still lifes, and take photographs for creating paintings. As usual, I always delayed the meals by taking endless photographs of the wine glasses and bottles, but my students soon got used to my antics, and learned how to take good photos as well.

The serene, foggy atmosphere of the Mendocino coast captivated us, and its spirit infused all our creative sessions. During the day, we'd take a break from class and hike out to photograph the field of white calla lilies on the headlands overlooking the ocean; from this time on, I was very inspired by the shapes of calla lilies, and included them in many paintings.

At first, many of the women were reluctant to take part in the communal hot tubs and sauna in the village, but by the end of the week, they were all enjoying themselves, chatting and rubbing honey-and-salt masques on their faces just like my Russian girlfriends in Moscow.

Mendocino is still a big part of my life. It is beautiful in any season, and when I'm there, I am full of creative energy. In the evenings, when I'm working alone, I gather all my sketches and photographs and create compositions for new paintings. The beauty of nature, the ocean, and the sunsets in the isolated north-coast town inspire me so much that after every visit, I come home filled with renewed energy and new ideas for my silk paintings.

Misha began to look forward to our mushrooming forays as much as I did. Like all parents, Steve and I think our child is very special, but Misha surprises us with new aspects of his developing personality every time we turn around. He's part standup comedian and part scientist, part budding artist and just plain boy.

Once when my co-author, Jeanne-Michele, came to my studio to see my slides of Russia, Misha, always the impresario, decided to take charge of the narration, interspersing silly laughter—"Look, here's Mummy falling down in the snow again!"—with the strangely wise comments of a child: "Look, here's the river. The water is flowing from the past into the future."

With Mom involved in painting every day, Misha's artistic side has been free to emerge, and he draws and paints endlessly. As I'm cleaning out the back seat of our car, I'll find elaborate diagrams: most recently, plans for a dolphin-shaped spaceship that fires sushi at its enemies. A few months ago, when I told him I was tired of painting the same images and needed some new inspiration, Misha said, "Don't worry, Mom, I'll make the designs for you, and you just paint them!"

I now have several capes and scarves with Misha's designs on them, and he's happy to be a part of my work, which unfortunately takes me away from him quite often for shows and classes.

Soon he'll be a moody teenager, so we're enjoying the last years of his innocence as much as we can.

Teaching art to children has always been an important part of my life. When I taught at Pioneer camps in Russia, I saw that during their three months' stay, the children were transformed by their experiences, coming away from my classes with new opinions about art and artists, as well as respect for their own paintings and drawings. Although I was reprimanded for introducing them to Modigliani and Chagall, I saw that kids could relate to the work of the forbidden modern painters at a very early age.

These days, when I'm teaching very small children at Starbright, a Russian-language preschool, I have great fun, delighting in my students' flights of fancy and blissful unawareness of their raw talent.

At the Jewish Community Center in Palo Alto, I taught hundreds of kids to paint on silk. Through these students, I met many of the parents in the local Russian community. When they first arrived in the Bay Area, and before they could even speak English, these highly-educated engineers cleaned houses and delivered pizzas; but after several years of hard work, most of them now have jobs in high-tech companies in Silicon Valley.

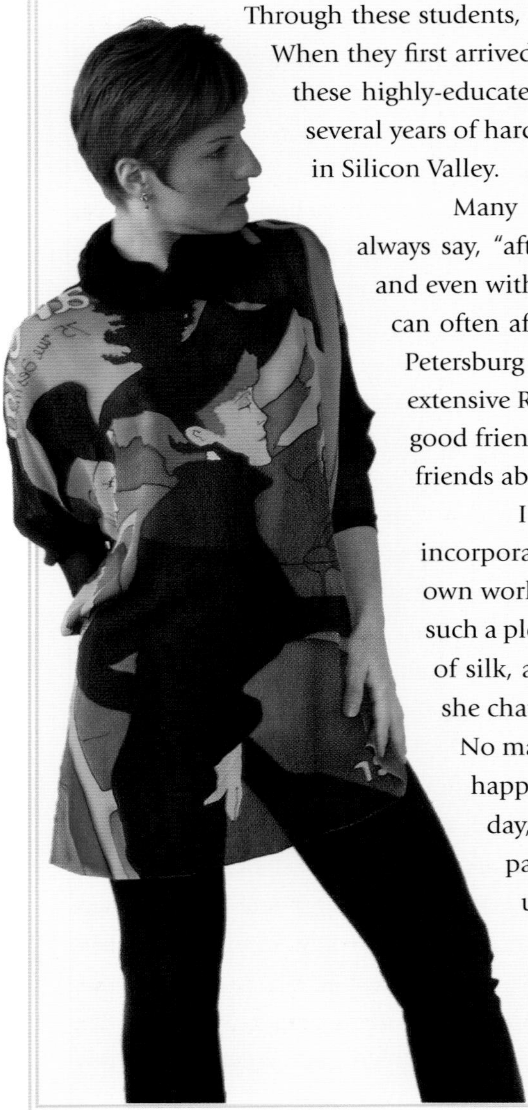

Many of these parents wanted to buy my paintings, but would always say, "after we buy a house. . ." Now they have all bought homes, and even with the ups and downs of the volatile high-tech economy, they can often afford to commission paintings of their favorite scenes of St. Petersburg and Europe. They are the core of my connection with the extensive Russian community in the South Bay, and many have become good friends, helping me to put on my fashion shows and telling their friends about my work.

I love the work of my favorite fine artists so much that I incorporate images in their painting styles, as well as scenes from my own work, into wearable art pieces, especially capes and scarves. It is such a pleasure to see a customer wrapped in a flowing, colorful piece of silk, a Toulouse-Lautrec cafe scene enhancing her own beauty as she chats at a party or opera intermission.

No matter where I am or what I'm doing, being an artist makes me happy. When I wake up each morning, I am excited as I greet the day, knowing I will soon be in my studio working on another painting. Even two days away from my dyes and brushes is uncomfortable.

Now I can afford to travel. But on vacations, I'm never just sitting on the beach or relaxing by a pool, although I am always ready to dive into the ocean waves and swim to the rocks. My trips are all working vacations, since at least half of the time I am busy with my camera, shooting material for my next series of paintings. Without exaggerating, I can say that I consider myself to be one of the luckiest people in the world.

Two years ago, I was invited to teach a group of fiber artists at the Textile Art Forum in Mittagong, Australia, and was thrilled at the opportunity to explore the Great Barrier Reef, where I shot underwater film of the coral paradise. Soon after my return, I painted several pieces on two layers of silk—half the painting on semi-opaque silk chiffon, and the other half on silk crepe de chine, so that each side of the reversible, framed work brought a different part of the underwater scene into sharp focus.

With my home studio, I enjoy having no separation between my job and the rest of my life. Everyone in the family knows that when I climb the narrow stairway to my attic retreat, I have "gone to work," and must not be disturbed. Yet I have enough experience and confidence so that after running errands, making dinner, or helping Misha with an art project, I can return to my work and refocus with the concentration I need to make a great painting.

I am content with this new phase of my life, and look back fondly at the adventures and misadventures that led me to my current existence, which—in comparison to living in Russia—is like being at a vacation retreat every day. Life is perfect—well, almost. Once or twice a year, I receive a letter postmarked in Biarritz, which usually reads something like this:

My dearest Natasha,

I trust that this letter finds you in good health. We are fine. Maman has found a wonderful restaurant fifteen kilometers up the coast that we're sure you'd just love. Bavarel makes the best duck confit in all of France. Yes, darling, I know, you signed those useless Soviet divorce papers in Moscow, but they don't mean a thing to me, you will always be mine. Maman and I are just waiting for you to come to your senses and return home where you belong. You'll get tired of those boring Americans soon enough: they'll fête you and flatter you and then spit you out and go on to their next fad. Do write and tell me when you are flying back to us.

Your devoted Etienne

When I finish reading one of these hopelessly lunatic messages, I find an old metal bucket under the kitchen sink, and take the bucket, a packet of matches, and the letter upstairs to my studio and out onto the little balcony Steve built for me. I crumple up the pages, light them, and watch as the letter turns into an ashy white residue. Then I toss the ashes out into the treetops in my back yard, and watch as the white wisps drift out toward San Francisco Bay. I take a deep breath, smile, and hope that my words are carried on the wind back to Etienne like the ashes from his letter, and I whisper, "In your dreams, Etienne. . . in your dreams."

Technique

It is hard to paint foliage on silk without being boring, and nothing reveals a painting to be the work of an amateur more than the indiscriminate use of emerald green. It is the enemy of the professional artist, who must search for any possible way not to use it, or at least change it to tones with only a little green in them, such as olives, tans, grays and golds.

In "Mendocino Highlands," I chose only the really important leaves in my photograph to fill the foreground with interesting shapes. First, I drew all the leaves with pencil, and then I outlined those closest to the viewer with resist. Calla lily leaves tend to fold themselves in half, so I represented each of those halves with a light and a dark section of the leaf, each outlined with resist. And I put a soft shadow in each of the light areas to add depth.

Figuring out how to color the rest of the leaves is like creating a jigsaw puzzle, making sure that too many same-toned leaves are not side by side. I painted the remaining leafy areas first in a light green, so that when I outlined individual leaves with resist, their shapes would recede. I painted some of the leaves in tones of red to make something interesting out of the mass of green; but even more importantly, there is red in the background, and I had to put warmer tones in the foreground to keep the background red from jumping out.

The calla lilies are not a true white in nature, since they reflect color from other objects around them, and I must study my photograph first to decide what pale tones to add to the calla lily blooms. To add light shadows, as pale as possible, in and under the cup of the flower heads, I created several shadow hues, let them dry out, and then wet the flowers, adding only the tiniest bit of dried-out dye when the section was slightly damp. Then I blended the shadows in.

And finally, I eliminated most of the architectural detail, and only hinted at it in places, to help the background recede into the distance.

Mendocino Highlands

24 Epilogue

Jeanne-Michele Salander, co-author

At a weekend silk-painting retreat in 1999, I listened with twelve other enthralled students as Natasha showed us slides of her paintings and told stories about her life. Her talent was breathtaking enough, but we found ourselves just as fascinated by her travels and adventures. When one woman joked, "Tell us when the book comes out," Natasha replied that she had always wanted to write her stories, but her English wasn't good enough, and she would need someone to help her. Naively clueless about the commitment I was just about to make, I offered to be her co-author.

I had been looking for the perfect book project for years, thinking that I wanted to make a collection of personal stories in the style of Studs Terkel. But this was even better: as an accomplished silk painter myself, I was deeply engaged with the medium. Moreover, I had studied Russian language and history in college with an inspiring professor, Robert Lewis, whose exceptionally accurate Russian accent fooled natives into thinking he was one of them. After thirty-five years, I still kept all my Russian books together in a hallowed spot on my bookshelves, along with notebooks of handwritten exercises in my careful Cyrillic script.

I especially loved to hear women speak Russian: it sounded like a bunch of softly-warbling mother birds that were discussing their fledglings' clumsiness as they tried to leave the nest. But I had abandoned any notion of being able to continue my Russian studies, as life had required me to be more practical, putting bread on the table for over twenty-five years as an in-house salesperson for Exotic Silks, a well-known silk importing business.

Over the course of five years, Natasha and I met for brief weekly meetings, sandwiching our editing sessions between other activities in our busy lives wherever our paths crossed—in cafes, empty classrooms, or parked in cars. After I had transcribed Natasha's tapes onto my computer disk, we would spend several sessions editing until we were satisfied that the writing rang true. I soon realized that my challenge was to write about Natasha's life without inserting my own voice into the work. But the details of her life began to flood my brain: one night I dreamed I was a woman lying between rumpled bed sheets (literally a figure in one of her paintings), and then I stepped out of the frame into the streets of Moscow.

I learned how to ask questions of my friend—and ease up when necessary—about the details of her personal life, trying to be sensitive to her intense feelings as she related some of her own and her family's stories. We left many of these stories out of our narrative to protect her family's privacy. And when I included too many descriptions of Russian politics and history that so fascinated me, Natasha would line them out as well. We wanted to write the book entirely from Natasha's perspective as an artist who singlemindedly focused on her art.

As time went by, Natasha would often say, "When you come to Russia," or "We'll have to take a trip so you can see Suzdal yourself." By the summer of 2002, the timing was right for our journey.

Though I have always avoided traveling with organized tours, the only way that most foreign visitors could see Russia, until quite recently, was under the watchful eyes of droning Soviet Intourist guides who led their docile charges around while quoting statistics about the latest agricultural crop yields. Now that tourists could travel in Russia in relative freedom, I could finally replace the black and white images of massive military parades in Red Square with my own colorful memories, and in the process, understand Natasha better.

The first hot, sultry night in Moscow, I lay on the couch by the open window in Zoya's living room, a lace curtain only partially blocking the endless mid-summer evening light. I could hear the sounds of the great city around me: several gun shots rang out, and there was the sound of drunken singing from a loud party. Cigarette smoke drifted up from the balcony of another sleepless resident below.

I could feel the energy of the Russian people as I envisioned the huge expanse of the Eurasian continent and the stunning panorama of events that its great authors—Dostoevsky, Tolstoy, Pasternak—had brought to life in their works.When I am jet-lagged, my imagination always runs wild until I finally flop, exhausted, into my bed.

Zoya had rented her apartment to me and my American traveling companion, Audrey, but she was hardly the absentee landlord: our gracious new friend kept popping in from her dacha (really a small farm a short train ride outside the city) with parcels of country cheese, fresh-squeezed blackberry juice, a thermos full of chokecherries she had picked, or some *kvass*, the homemade beer that Russians drank in enormous quantities in the summertime.

Our first foray into central Moscow included a visit to Red Square, which was far bigger than I had imagined; the red-brick Kremlin walls were impossibly high. Tears welled in my eyes as I thought, *I'm finally here.* Bob Lewis would be so proud of me—he always insisted his students must go to Russia some day.

St. Basil's Cathedral, the familiar symbol from travel posters, loomed in the background. No longer an image on paper made of colored inks, it was solid and bulky, its badly-decaying red, green and white domes draped with restoration scaffolding. And as I stared around myself in awe, I heard the millions of footsteps that had trod these red bricks, and remembered the military parades, the uniformed Soviet leaders saluting stiffly from the top of Lenin's tomb.

Red Square was now thronged with Russians who dressed in the latest fashions and posed for photos like visitors in any European city. And at the north end of the square, a tiny open-air chapel that had been taken down by Stalin to make way for the parades of tanks and missiles was now restored in brilliantly-painted hues. A small group of women, young and old, stood under a gilded cornice, scarves reverently tied over their hair, while a priest intoned evening prayers.

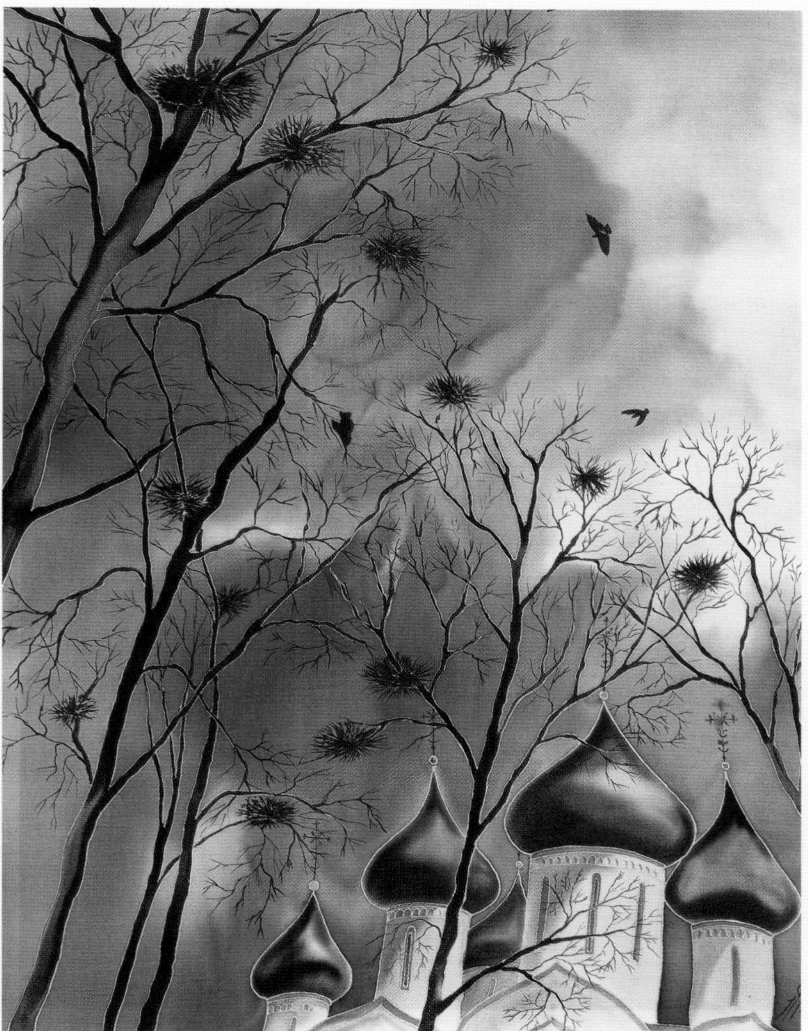

On the way to the Pushkin Museum the next day, Audrey and I picked souvenir leaves from the apple trees in the backyard of Tolstoy's Moscow residence, and had lunch in one of Moscow's most elegant restaurants, the Grand Imperial. For the price of an elderly Russian's monthly pension check, we dined on a delicious *"biznizmiens"* lunch of hearty beef soup, fresh salad, a half-bottle of vintage French Bordeaux, and mushroom piroshkis served on antique china and glassware. In the background, a musician played New York show tunes on a grand piano that displayed a signed photo of last year's guests, the Rolling Stones. Later we learned that the Grand Imperial was a favorite hangout of Boris Yeltsin's daughter.

The Pushkin was a world-class museum, not so large as to be overwhelming, but stuffed with art treasures. I found the architectural models of the Acropolis where Etienne had first started a conversation with Natasha, and made my pilgrimage alone to the Roman Architecture Hall, where Natasha had the out-of-body experience in "Flight." Sadly, the room was roped off and closed "for technical reasons"; but as I peered into the silent space, the gloomy, green-tinged room, with its busts of marble Roman heads peering out at me, held me spellbound for several minutes, and I, too, almost felt myself lifting into the air and out the glass ceiling.

Dima's old apartment building stood, just as Natasha had described it, across the street from the pleasant grounds of the museum. Sadly, however, developers had discovered its fine old architecture, and workers were gutting out the insides of the structure to make it into an office building.

Natasha and her family had arrived in Suzdal the day before us, so Audrey and I took the bus there by ourselves. We saw no other foreign women traveling alone anywhere on our trip, and when several Russians told us they only saw women like us in organized tour groups, we felt really proud of our independence.

In Suzdal, we joined Steve, Natasha, and the two Mishas for a delicious meal in the dining hall of a restored monastery. After several sips of straight vodka (I knew better than to try downing shots), the buzz hit me; I wasn't loosely relaxed as I would have been if drinking wine, but paralyzed, as if shot by a zoo-keeper's stun gun. I watched, transfixed, as the waiters took breaks outside a huge carved wooden doorway in the endless evening light. Each new pose as they sat and smoked was like another Impressionist painting, reduced to just the basics: the pale lemon-yellow sky, the lush brilliant green of trees, the black pants, the white shirts—no superfluous details. I remembered Vasin telling his students that vodka slows you down so you can really see, and he was right.

Natasha was taking pictures of brass samovars and wine glasses on a broad windowsill with a barred window and a garden in the background, and I followed suit, taking multiple shots of the waiters. Then, I gathered all my concentration and attempted a toast in praise of Russia: "I've been to France, to Italy, to China, and to Mexico, but I've never seen anything as beautiful as Suzdal on a summer's evening."

Misha, ever the wry poet, responded with that ironic black humor that Russians have mastered through generations of hardship: "I've been in Lefortovo (a prison), the Lubianka (a prison), and Kresty (another prison), and I have enough memories to last a lifetime!"

At the end of the meal, I drank a cup of Russian black tea to overcome the effects of the vodka, but it was a big mistake, because the tea was so strong that I couldn't sleep at all.

Audrey and I had booked two nights in the Pokrovsky Convent, and as I lay sleepless on my narrow twin bed under starched white sheets, the golden domes and white walls of the convent church glimmered in floodlights outside my window, punctuated by a red icon of an unknown saint over the doorway. I lay under the church's spell all night, its presence like a person's. At first I enjoyed the aura of serenity as I contemplated Suzdal's peaceful beauty; but after many sleepless hours, I was desperate, and began praying to the icon's saint to take pity on me and bring me sleep. At about five in the morning, I finally dozed off.

The next day Suzdal presented her sleepy charms: cows grazing in lush green water meadows and the long-skirted girl who tended them, knitting socks as she watched; onion-domed churches gracing every horizon; children riding horses along the ramparts; people sitting around little camp fires, relaxing in the cool evening air. I wanted to be there in the winter, to be taken everywhere by a horse-drawn sleigh, to sit by my fireplace on snowy nights and knit like a Russian cowgirl. It was a fantasy, but a potent one. Something in Suzdal made me want to stay forever, its calm a refuge from our scary world.

My limited Russian vocabulary had proved invaluable in Moscow, because I could read signs in Cyrillic and navigate us around the subway system. Now we would have an even bigger adventure: we would take the train to St. Petersburg by ourselves while Natasha prepared for her show of silk paintings in Moscow.

All my romantic notions of train travel flooded my mind on the six-hour journey: the trains in Dr. Zhivago, the Orient Express. Lulled half asleep by the clacking rhythm of metal wheels on train tracks, I would go out into the passageway, stand by the open window, and watch the dizzy progression of trees, fields, ponds, fences, the sky. The Volga River was as wide as a lake, stretching out to the horizon. On my way to the dining car, I picked my way quickly through a cluster of belligerent, drunken soldiers. Yet when I carelessly left my travel journal behind with the empty dishes, a young man ran through five train cars to give it back to me.

Just as Natasha had written in "St. Petersburg," women doctors and teachers talked openly with us on the train. Their relatively comfortable lives had been shattered by the wrecked economy; many were now jobless, with no promise of a future for their children. One woman, a speech therapist, reached out to close the door to our compartment before we continued the conversation: was she fearful that the staff was still informing on Russians talking to foreigners, or was it just a habit from the old days?

Natasha had arranged for an extremely reasonable and nicely remodeled apartment for Audrey and me, complete with kitchen utensils, hairdryer, and a radio. It was so inexpensive that we could afford one of St. Petersburg's best guides, Eugenia Snopkovskaya. A former rhythmic gymnast, Eugenia walked with such perfect posture and had such excellent table manners that she put us both to shame. Granddaughter of a Cossack hero of the Great War, she had mastered four languages, studied at Oxford, and now took extra classes at the Hermitage to increase her knowledge of its art treasures. She was also skilled at the fine art of avoiding lines, and slipped past hordes of people like a graceful ferret, getting us coveted reservations to see the Scythian gold treasures on our first try. We would have been hopelessly lost without her in the Hermitage's 1,057 rooms.

I was struck dumb by St. Petersburg's lavish palaces and art treasures, so to keep from going into an "art coma," I took a cue from Natasha, and focused on the beauty of small scenes in unexpected places. Jogging to keep up with Audrey and Eugenia, the Energizer travel bunnies, I stopped to take photos like my mentor: reflections in water; a marble statue of a baby in a huge seashell—the marble reflecting the colors of objects around it, just like Natasha had said it would. I want to return to St. Petersburg again and again, to spend months there. I would even submit to a tour or a cruise to get back to all that beauty and history.

In grammar school, I had to write reports with titles like "Colombia, Land of Many Contrasts." But in the international "many contrast" contest, Russia wins hands down. The great nation was bigger than life, yet intimate like a series of villages—richer than I could ever have imagined, yet poor

as dirt away from the major cities. The people were gruff and suspicious of foreigners, but once they heard me struggling to speak Russian, they were gracious and generous.

In the Armory Palace behind the Kremlin walls, we saw diamond treasures that left us speechless: gigantic necklaces and crowns; a horse blanket studded with thousands of gems; a map of the Soviet Union made of diamonds; buckets of loose stones. The room displaying them was an actual vault, with armed guards at the entrance, and only one way out.

Although there was an abundance of excellent food, the higher-priced restaurants, decorated like a Viking lair or an Uzbek yurt, were mostly empty. But to combat the endless, snowy winters, Russian cooks had mastered the art of soup-making, and inexpensive self-serve cafes now offered a huge variety of choices: fish soups, mushroom soups, beef soups rich with homemade broth and topped with dollops of sour cream and fresh dill. A rust belt of deserted factories and ugly concrete high-rises ringed Moscow, while glass-fronted buildings in modern neighborhoods towered over elderly berry vendors on pensions, gypsies in dirty, brightly-colored skirts, and sleek SUVs disgorging well-heeled passengers and their gun-toting drivers. A drunk soldier lay senseless outside the train station, his arm bleeding from a knife wound. No one paid him any attention.

I was stripped of any notions of Russia as a bleak, second-rate country. It was certainly having its troubles, again, but it is a rich and a great country. How ironic that the Soviet authorities fooled Natasha and her Komsomol Youth groups with movies of Americans standing in Depression bread lines, while our government used the same propaganda, showing us Eisenhower-era kids only newsreels of Russians standing in their bread lines!

What filled my heart the most was awe at the Russian people's survival skills. They had lived through hundreds of years of serfdom under an insanely wealthy nobility, undergone a major revolution, and lost millions to World War II and Stalin's purges. The fully modern nation was now an ecological disaster. A new gang of wealthy Russians, the "kleptocracy," had grabbed control of Russia's vast oil and natural gas industries, while ordinary people just kept trying to make ends meet.

I came home with a journal full of travel notes from my trip, and tons of photographs. When I look at my photos now, the experience is as fresh in my memory as if I had gone last week.

Writing *Silk Diary* and experiencing Russia first-hand has been a journey of discovery for me. Furthermore, I now have a different kind of respect for Natasha. I had always admired her artistic skills, but now I saw the courage underlying her crazy adventures, and the solidness of her determination to be an artist, undeterred by economic need, romance, or the vodka flasks of her bohemian art student days.

As Natasha and I worked on this final chapter, sitting in her car, Misha drew pictures in the back seat; Mom was taking him to the dentist after we had completed our edits for the week. The dark-haired nine-year-old with the merry eyes and enigmatic smile asked, "Why are you writing this book now? An autobiography is about someone's life, and Mom's only forty, she's not dead yet!" You can always count on children to ask the direct questions.

"Well, Misha," Natasha laughed, "we'll be too old to write the rest of the story, so you'll have to write the second volume for us: "Natasha: The Later Years. . ."

His eyes had the distant, unfocused look I always got when I was dreaming up images and plot lines for the next chapter of *Silk Diary*. Perhaps Misha will take over my place in front of the computer screen. We'll see.

List of Suppliers

Silk Painting Materials

Atelier de Paris
1543 So. Robertson Blvd.
Los Angeles, CA 90035
phone: (310) 553-6636 • fax: (310) 553-9621
email: rosemary@atelierdeparis.com
www.atelierdeparis.com
Silk painting supplies.

Dharma Trading Co.
P. O. Box 150916
San Rafael, CA 94915
phone: 1-800-542-5227 • fax: (415) 456-8747
www.dharmatrading.com
Textile crafts supplies and garment blanks.

Exotic Silks
1959 Leghorn St.
Mtn. View, CA 94043
phone: 1-800-845-7455 • fax: (650) 965-0712
email: silks@exoticsilks.com
www.exoticsilks.com
Silk yardage, scarf and garment blanks.

Pro Chemical and Dye Co.
P. O. Box 14
Somerset, MA 02726
phone: 1-800-228-9393 • fax: (508) 676-3980
email: promail@prochemical.com
www.prochemical.com
Dyes and related supplies, classes.

Qualin International Inc.
P. O. Box 31145
San Francisco, CA 94131
phone: (415) 970-8888 • fax:(415) 282-8789
email: silk@qualinsilk.com
web: www.qualinsilk.com
Silk painting supplies.

Rupert Gibbon & Spider
P. O. Box 425
Healdsburg, CA 95448
phone:1-800-442-0455 • fax: (707) 433-4906
www.jacquardproducts.com
Dyes, paints, accessories, kits.

Thai Silks
252 State St.
Los Altos, CA 94022
phone: (650) 948-8611 • fax: (650) 948-3426
email: silks@thaisilks.com
www.thaisilks.com
Silk fabrics, scarf and garment blanks.

Things Japanese
9805 N. E. 116th St., PMB 7160
Kirkland, WA 98034
phone: (425)-821-2287 • fax: (425)-821-3554
email: thesilkexperience@silkthings.com
www.silkthings.com
Silk thread, non-toxic instant set dyes.

Check Your Local Bookstore or Order Here

Please send me_______copies of *Silk Diary* for $39.95 each.

Include $6.05 shipping and handling for one book; a flat rate of $8.10 for 2-4 books. Larger orders will be shipped by UPS Ground. Canadian orders must be made in U.S. funds. California residents add 8.5% sales tax.

Payment must accompany orders. Allow 3 weeks for delivery.

My check or money order for **$**_____________ is enclosed.
Make payable to Winter Palace Press.

Please charge my: ❑ Visa ❑ MasterCard ❑ American Express

Name ____

Organization____

Address____

City/State/Zip _______________________________________

Phone ____________________ E-mail ___________________________

Card # ____

Expiration Date ____________ Signature___________________________

To contact us call: 1-877-848-2240
Send payment to:

WINTER PALACE PRESS
1690 HAYES STREET, SAN FRANCISCO, CA 94117
www.winterpalacepress.com